La Jefa

Stephanie K. Randall

For
The Readers of Living Fast and The Return of
Ms. Rose

Copyright 2015 by Stephanie K. Randall

All Rights Reserved.

"You are la jefa... That means you are the boss... Everything in this house flows through you. Keep building your empire. A worthy man will come along and be everything that you need him to be... Trust me."

ACKNOWLEDGEMENTS

First and foremost, I would like to thank my Lord and Savior Jesus Christ for everything that He has done. I want to thank my mother Bridgett Tucker for being there for me as always. I would also like to thank my children Sanaa and Shiloh for keeping me motivated. I would like to thank all of my family for supporting me and cheering me on with every book that I release. I do not take it lightly. There are a lot of people who don't have a support system, but I do and I am grateful for that. I would also like to thank my other half Mr. Christopher Jones, for being the wonderful man that he is. He has shown me real love and support which makes my life even more rewarding. Last but certainly not least I want to send a special thank you to ALL of my loyal readers who have been reading since day one! I LOVE YOU ALL! Xoxoxoxo... The best is yet to come.

TABLE OF CONTENTS

CHAPTER 1: A Rose Is Still A Rose..1
CHAPTER 2: Business As Usual...6
CHAPTER 3: I Love Him But I Hate Him............................13
CHAPTER 4: Still Trying... But He's Stupid.......................20
CHAPTER 5: A Storm Is Brewing...32
CHAPTER 6: Not So Happy Holiday.....................................43
CHAPTER 7: Checks..50
CHAPTER 8: Photo shoot..58
CHAPTER 9: The Last Straw..63
CHAPTER 10: Papi Knows Best...73
CHAPTER 11: I Still Got It...83
CHAPTER 12: Paul...90
CHAPTER 13: This Girl * Rolls Eyes *................................100
CHAPTER 14: The Cat Is Out The Bag..............................105
CHAPTER 15: Meeting Nesha..112
CHAPTER 16: Self Evaluation..118
CHAPTER 17: Change of Heart..123
CHAPTER 18: Love Will Make You Stupid.......................134
CHAPTER 19: The Straw That Broke the Camels Back........140
CHAPTER 20: The Best Way to Get Over the Other One...
    Is With Another One..147
CHAPTER 21: Everything Happens for a Reason.................157
CHAPTER 22: Reflecting and Moving Forward...................167

CHAPTER 1
A Rose Is Still A Rose

I am a woman
if I am not anything else
I bleed and I cry
just like everybody else
I'm a real woman
I have my flaws
Perfect I am not
But my insecurities I try my best to keep on pause
There are always struggles in life
Many valleys and peaks
But I've made up my mind to embrace it all
To stand tall and not accept defeat
For the ending result of my decisions
They all start with me
This life it is mine
I determine how successful I'm going to be
Not crying no rivers and no pity parties
This woman here is far from pitiful

This lady here
is a strong independent boss
And her blessings have been plentiful
Since I have changed my life
And placed myself on a higher plane
There have been those who have chosen to hate
Which I feel is a bitter and ugly shame
But I can't control their emotions or opinions for that matter
I know for sure who and what I am
I can brush off my shoulder and ignore the negativity
I have no need for making scenes or going h.a.m.
Not unless it involves my family or my money
Then I may have to revert to the pork
Yes Ms. Rose can be as sweet as honey
Until you try to snatch the food from her fork
Growing up I never would have thought
That little old me would be building

an empire of my own
With a car for every day of the week
With a pool, basketball court, and marble floors in my home
I have come a long way
From depending on a man to feed me
To making decisions and calling the shots
And having the means to provide for my whole family
From ducking in alleys
And strolling in death's valley
To shiny red coupes
And tailored white suits
I look up at the sky
And I ask God what did I do to deserve all of this
Then he reminds me why
When I continue to reminisce
On what the barrel of a gun looked like
When it stared me in my face
Or when I wandered the streets
Without a stable place to stay

Every stripe I have earned
So I find it safe to say
That God saved a wretch like me
And showed me a new way
By giving me security and stability
I can not begin to thank Him enough
Because I remember the days
When just waking up was tough
And I was blind to the suns bright rays
I lived in darkness
And dealing with my mother's death was the hardest
And largest pill that I thought I would never be able to digest
But look at me now
Receiving the best of the best
And it feels so good to know
What the bottom looks and feels like
Because it gave me the opportunity to grow
So to anybody who feels like
They can't make it through the day
Just know that I know what that feels

like
But I made it
And you can do the same
Not saying that it will be easy
But if you want it
Put in the work
That's much more rewarding
Then wallowing in your past hurts
I'm not trying to preach
I'm not trying to boast
I'm just a woman who knows
Life that's not all cream mixed with peach
But I also know
That true happiness
Is not too far from your reach
So just like I'm telling you
Sometimes I have to repeat to me
A rose is still a rose
Even when it's smashed between concrete.

CHAPTER 2
Business As Usual

I took a sip of my coffee, then took a deep breath. This dude really had to be kidding me.

"So what you're saying is that you want to pay my client two thousand dollars?"

"Yes, I feel like that's good for the job," Mr. Milli said.

"Hum. I see. Well, are you aware that my client is a super model? She is not a video vixen. Now I'm not trying to discredit anyone in that profession. Everyone has their own lane. But, Violet has walked down runways in Paris. She has been on the cover of Elle. Two thousand dollars just isn't acceptable," I replied.

"OK, well that's my final offer," he snapped back.

"Well I'm going to have to respectfully decline. I wish you the best in your future endeavors."

Right before I hung up I heard him murmur the word, "bitch". It didn't ruffle my feathers at all though. It came with the territory. In this business, there was always a man trying to go toe to toe with me, and I gladly accepted the challenge. I am a boss, and I have earned this title. H.B.I.C. Head Boss In Charge. Therefore, what I say goes. I had been constantly put in positions where I had to exercise my authority, because men would always try me. Furthermore, it was clear to me what his problem was. "Mr. Milli" was used to women drooling at the chance to be in his artist's videos. Being the manager of a hot rap artist had the potential to blow a nigga's head up quick. Sadly, the type of money that they were trying to pay wasn't sufficient for the caliber of model that Violet was. I wasn't going to short change her just so that she could be the "leading lady" in a Young Bread video. I could see right through that whole operation that they were running over there. Clearly "Mr. Milli" didn't possess as many millions as his name portrayed, and Young Bread's name suggested exactly the type of bread that he had. Young baby money. Two thousand dollars couldn't even pay half of the mortgage on Violet's condo, so she wouldn't be missing a thing.

7

    I pulled up Young Bread's most recent video on my cell phone. "Money Never End" was what it was called. I laughed at the title alone. After shaking the laughter off, I began to watch. It was so typical. Girls with huge asses shaking everywhere. Young Bread bopping around holding stacks of money with his skin tight pants basically down to his ankles and dudes sitting around a table trying to look hard. I shook my head. This was something that I just could not understand. What is the point of putting on a pair of pants that suffocated your balls just to sag them off your ass? What was the whole point of having your pants hanging off your ass anyway? Gosh that video had taken four and a half minutes away from my life that I could never get back.

    I glanced back over at my email at the so called "treatment" of the video that Violet that had been requested for, which by the way was entitled, "That's My Bitch". For radio purposes the title had been changed to "That's My Chic." Anyway, nothing about it was original. Straight boring. Another Bonnie and Clyde type of deal, but with Violet wearing skimpy clothes. Nope. I didn't want her anywhere near this "video". As a matter of fact, I didn't want her anywhere near him at all. That little boy was bad news. She wasn't missing out on a thing. I was more than happy to let this one pass her by.

    I chuckled and shrugged my shoulders as I dialed Leandro's number. Now let me fill yall in on Leandro. He was a fine ass puerto rican model that I had been managing for about seven months at that time. Work needed to be done on the bathroom at my house. Well I wanted a new bathroom. So we hired a group of contractors and when they came to the house, the first thing I noticed was the extremely handsome young man that stood out from the rest of the crew.

"You should be a model," I told him hoping that he spoke English.

"Oh... Nooo.. I work. That's all," he responded heavily accented.

"Of course you do. But being a model is work too. Here, take my card," I said sliding it into his pocket.

  Leandro and his uncles finished the work on my bathroom and that was that. Or so I thought. About four months later I got an unexpected call. It was Leandro. He had a falling out with one of his uncles that he did work with and now he didn't have a source of income. He wanted to hear a little more about what I could do for him as far as introducing him to the modeling world. I was ecstatic. He would be my first male client. And as I mentioned before he was absolutely positively gorgeous. Chiseled cheek bones, golden brown skin, extremely dark curly ear length hair, and broad shoulders. And man oh man when this guy took off his shirt it was like his body was handcrafted by Picasso himself. Pecs on point. Biceps... Lord have mercy. Triceps... Spectacular. And his abs. Oh my God his abs. There were one, two, three, four, five, six, seven, eight... Yup, we call that an eight pack. Yes indeed, he would be a money maker for sure.

  Anyway, I called Leandro to set up a lunch date for us. There was plenty that we needed to speak about. He had been offered a Calvin Klein underwear deal, which in itself was a huge deal. I was blown away with all the positive responses that I had received about Leandro. His career had sky rocketed from zero to one hundred in no time, just as Violet's had. After speaking with Leandro, I was ready to make my way home.

  Just as I shut my laptop down, my desk phone rang. I looked at the caller I.D. It was Violet.
"Hey girl I was just talking about you a little while ago."
"About what and to who?"
"Well you know the rapper Young Muffin?"
"You mean Young Bread?"
"Yeah. Whatever. Him. Anyway, his manager who calls himself Mr. Milli, contacted me. He was trying to get you to be in that boy's video."
"Really? So when is it?" Violet asked.
"Doesn't matter. I declined," I said.
"Why?"
"Because he was only trying to pay you two thousand dollars

Violet. That's not wassup. At all."

"But you didn't even ask me," Violet said defensively.

"Since when have I had to consult you when I book you for stuff? Refresh my memory because I don't think that has happened.. Like never," I shot back.

"Umm."

"Umm what? It is my job to get you the most money and the best exposure possible Violet. Not to book you for music videos with rat face boys with minimal funds."

"You're crazy Rosie. He does not look like a rat," Violet giggled.

"Well what he look like then? Because he ain't cute, that's for sure."

"Yes he is."

"Oh nope. I don't like where this conversation is going. You are sounding like a groupie. You make too much money to be a groupie Violet. Cut it out," I scolded her.

"So saying he's cute makes me a groupie?"

"I'm not about to go back and forth with you about him. You're not doing the video. And let me take this a step further by saying you need to stay away from him too. Because I can feel your googly eyes through the phone."

"Whatever Rosie I don't even know him," Violet replied.

"Yeah OK. Well keep it that way."

"OK."

"I'm serious Violet I see him all over the internet with all these different women he's a straight up hoe," I continued to warn her.

"Oh my gosh please just leave it alone Rosie... Well in other news... I was calling to let you know that this virgin hair company reached out to me. They want me on board. I gave them your info so you can work it out."

"Oh OK. That sounds good! Everybody and their grandmother wears hair nowadays. So that's gonna be a good move. But look, I'm trying to get out of here I want to go home and try to relax. So I'll talk to you later," I said.

"Ard. Bye."

I hung up the phone, gathered my things, then made my way on home. I pulled into the drive way and let out a sigh of a relief. My bed was calling my name. LOUDLY. I was greeted with the smell of burning cheese as soon as I hit the door. I shook my head and dropped my briefcase in the foyer, then I made my way to the kitchen. There Deon stood in front of the stove, spatula in hand.
"Deon, what are you doing?" I asked him.
"Fixing a grilled cheese," he answered.
"It smells like you're burning it," I replied taking the spatula from him.

I looked in the pan and rolled my eyes. Grilled cheese? Nah. More like a burned blacker than the street cheese. I dumped the ruined sandwich in the trash and placed the pan in the sink.
"You had the flame too high," I enlightened him.
"Oh. Well I was hungry and I didn't know when you were coming in," Deon remarked.
"Deon I texted you. You knew I was on my way."
"Well shit I didn't know how long you were gonna take, you got a habit of taking your time."
"Whatever," I said placing a clean pan onto the stove.

I grabbed the loaf of bread from the breadbox and then two slices of cheese from the refrigerator.
"I wouldn't have to try to cook if you were home," Deon complained.
"Well I'm not a house wife Deon. I am a career woman. When I am here, I cook. When I'm not I can't. Anyway, I told you that there were a few things already in the refrigerator. All you had to do was warm it up."
"I didn't want leftovers."

See now I was ready to go upside his head. This dude had it all the way screwed up. All I wanted to do was go out and make my own money. After my situation with Marlon years ago, I never wanted to give a man control over my finances again. Just because Deon was my husband didn't make him any different. I had to get up, get out, and get something.

The stay at home Jan Brady type of life just didn't fit me. Now don't get me wrong, I loved to take care of my family. And even though I stayed on the go, I still managed to keep my family in tact. But Deon was just being a dick. Flat out.
"F.Y.I. They are not *leftovers*. They are meals that I prepared and put away so that you wouldn't have to try to cook when I'm not here."
"Sounds like leftovers to me," Deon replied.
    I took a deep breath and flipped the grilled cheese over in the pan.
"Why can't we just hire a personal chef?" Deon asked.
"Deon we already had this conversation. I don't have a problem with it as long as it is a man."
"I mean but what difference does it make?"
"Oh you know what difference it makes," I shot back.
    I had been naive before, but that wouldn't happen again. I had forgiven Deon but I most certainly did not forget. So having a woman in my house while I wasn't home was never going to happen again. NEVER. I didn't care how Deon felt about it. The life lesson of never trusting a woman around your man will stick with me for the rest of my life.
    I slid the grilled cheese on to the plate then sliced it in half. It was perfect. Golden brown and the cheese was melted evenly. I was the shit in my eyes. Three successful businesses and I could still come straight home from my office and hook up a perfect grilled cheese in a blouse, pencil skirt, and heels.
"Here you go," I said placing the plate in front of Deon on the table. I filled a glass with some juice and put it beside his plate. He grabbed the glass and took a big gulp. That was it. No "thank you." No "I love you." No "how was your day?" I sucked it up and went to our bedroom. This attitude from Deon had become normal behavior. It was like nothing that I did was good enough for him and nothing that I did was ever acknowledged. Just like the time I went to the salon and got my hair lightened.. No response. When I lost ten pounds... No response. When I expanded the daycare center... No response. Or the time I baked him a pineapple upside down cake from

scratch because he said that he had always eaten cakes from a box... No response. When I was voted "Parent of the Month" by Miracle's class... No response. Even when I struck up the deal with Calvin Klein for Leandro... Still no response. Any other man would be proud to have a successful wife who also had good qualities outside of being a money maker. But it seemed to me like Deon felt threatened. I just didn't understand. He hadn't always been like this. There had been a time where it seemed like he genuinely wanted to see me win. But now it seemed like some weird type of competition. It was like if it didn't revolve around his career then it didn't matter much.

    I sat on my bed and began to ponder on my marriage as a whole. When Deon cheated on me with Michelle I was snatched back to reality. I thought about leaving him for good, but then I thought about my family. I didn't want to take my children or his children through another transition. Deon worked his ass off to get me back. And now, I had to be brutally honest with myself. I just wasn't happy. This was not what I had signed up for. This Deon was not the Deon that I married. He was always so critical of me. All I wanted to do was be successful and show my kids and husband how great I was. My kids seemed to get it. But my husband on the other hand I wasn't too sure.

    Well, I couldn't sit there and over analyze everything. I didn't have the time. I had to go get Miracle from ballet, Franko from boxing, and Summer from the daycare. A mother's job is never done. All these responsibilities were good at times, but then I felt a little overwhelmed at times. I might have felt a little rosier if had a little positivity brewing in my home's coffee pot. Every day I wondered to myself if things would get better with Deon. I still loved him. I was still in love with him. But being with him was sucking me dry.

    More times than often I would ask God if I would be wrong for leaving Deon. I couldn't decipher what His answer was though.

CHAPTER 3
I Love Him But I Hate Him

    I sat in my seat going over a few of the spread sheets on my laptop. This had been one of the very few days that I had to attempt to chill out a little bit. Yes, looking over my work was sort of a chill time for me. Anyway, I sipped my glass of champagne as the other wives chatted amongst themselves. I still wasn't big on being cliqued up with them. I would rather stay to myself. Le'Velle's wife had attempted to get close to me since she struck up Violet's first deal with me, but um- no. I wasn't having it. I wanted no parts of her whatsoever (unless it dealt with money). It seemed like they were a bunch of high school girls. Every other game somebody was mad with somebody or not speaking to one another. They pretended to be so close but it was clear that all they were doing was competing with each other. It was just too much drama that I didn't want anything to do with. I didn't need any distractions from the money that I already had, nor the money that I desired to make. The situation that I had with Mocha had really taught me a lesson. I was going to not only choose my battles wisely, but also avoid situations that could possibly put me in a position where I would have battles to face. I glanced over toward the field just in time. Deon was ready to throw the ball. But it wasn't looking good at all.
    I heard the loud crunch of the football equipment as I saw Deon being sacked. A chill went through my body and I screamed. I had seen him get hit before, but nothing like this. When Deon didn't get up, I knew that something was really wrong. I hopped up from my seat spilling my champagne everywhere and dropping my laptop to the floor. It seemed like it took forever for the medics to get on the field to tend to him. I just felt it in my gut. He was hurt pretty bad. The look on his face I will never forget. It was a look of excruciating pain. I ran down to get a closer look at what was happening. Deon's eyes were clenched shut as he was carried off the field. Wow.
    I watched ESPN from my phone as I sat in the waiting room. Everybody was talking about the same thing- Deon's

injury. I felt so bad for him. I knew this was going to be hard for him. He loved football so much and I knew that when something someone loves is taken away trouble soon follows.

My thoughts were interrupted by the head surgeon coming out to speak with me.

"The surgery went very well. He is waking up now. Once we get him settled in a bit, then we'll let you in to see him."

"Thank you," I responded.

I exhaled and released the tension from my shoulders. I was always nervous when I heard of people having to be put under anesthesia. I wiggled my butt a little deeper into my seat, and waited for the okay to go back to see my husband. Then I switched back into my thoughts. Our plans for Thanksgiving would definitely be different since Deon would be home recovering from his injury. I thought that he could use some love and family time, so I made a mental note to invite everybody over to our place for Thanksgiving dinner. This would be great! It had been a while since the whole family had gotten together. The last time my side and his side had been together was for Summers birthday. It had been way too long.

"Mrs. Matteo, you can come on back," was the next thing that I heard.

I followed the nurse back to Deon's room. My husband always had the most angelic look when he was in dreamland. I loved that man with every bone and breath in my body. I stared at him as his chest rose and fell. He couldn't possibly know how much I wanted our marriage to survive. I was so committed. Seeing him like this broke my heart. I kissed him gently on his lips and began to wake up.

"Well hey there," I said to Deon as his eyes opened.

Nothing was more important to me than being right there by my husband's side. I knew that this was difficult for him.

"Hi," he said still a little groggy from the anesthesia.

"So how do you feel sir?" I asked playfully.

"I'm ready to go."

"But baby you can't go yet. You just got out of recovery. They

will let you go as soon as-"
"I don't wanna hear all that. I'm ready to go home," Deon interrupted.
"Just get some rest," I said.
"Whatever," he snapped.

I could already see that this wasn't going to be a pleasant journey at all. Deon had a stank attitude ever since they pulled him off the field with that torn ACL. Well let me rephrase that. His attitude had been stank for the past few months, but it grew to an even higher level of stankness (I know that's not a real word) ever since he had been injured. For the past couple of days we had been going to specialists and surgeons exploring all of our possible options. His demeanor about the situation hadn't changed not one bit. Sure, life had given him a lemon or two… But there was so much that he could make from them. Lemon pie, lemonade, lemon cake, lemon cookies, lemon pepper wings, hell even a lemon drop. But of course Deon didn't see it that way. All I was trying to do was shoot some optimism his way. I guess that wasn't enough either. All I could do was write.

The funny thing about love is...
You can love a person so much that you can't stand them...
The crazy thing about love is...
One minute you're love birds...
The next you're arguing about things that are so random...
The awkward thing about love is...
You start doing things you said you'd never do...

The toughest thing about love is...
Contemplating if this love thing is really for you...
One minute you're up...
Then down the next...
You're not really sure of what to do...
Do you stick around and see it through?
Or do you let it go and say you're through?
sigh
Now what is this we're going through?
You said you were committed to me...
And I to you...
But now things just seem so broken...
You were just loving everything I do...
But now you twist the words that I have spoken...
You were just the beat of my heart...
But now all I wanna do is choke you...
I think we need some time apart...
I'm so confused...
My ego is bruised...

You said my role is beside you...
But sometimes I really don't know what's going on inside of you...
From the beginning I told you...
That I don't always act like I'm supposed to...
And I know that dealing with me can be hard...
But the things that we disagree about to me just seem so odd...
Now I'm not pointing fingers or placing blame...
I'm just letting you know that things aren't the same...
Maybe the realness of the situation is settling in...
Suddenly your patience with me wears thin...
You knew that you had a heart to mend...
Maybe this is too much for you...
Maybe I'm not all I'm cracked up to be...
Maybe you didn't think it through

when you said you wanted to marry me...
Maybe I'm just overreacting...
Guess we'll just have to wait and see...
A long time ago I learned...
Love isn't always peaches and cream...
Sometimes the ways of your mate will make you want to scream...
At others your need for their love is reminiscent of a fiend...
And then all the time in between can go either way...
I know they say that love cannot be a street that is one way...
I just need to know that I am your first place...
I need to know that in your heart I am secure in that place...
Because just yesterday I was your ace...
But today...
I don't even want to see your face...
I don't know if you'll hold that against me...

Or throw that statement in my face...
Or if this is just another disagreement that will disappear without a trace...
The funny thing about love is...
You can love a person so much that you can't stand them...
The crazy thing about love is...
One minute you're love birds...
The next you're arguing about things that are so random...

How could he be so mean and nasty to me? All I was trying to do was be there for him in his time of need. All I was trying to do was be a good wife to him. That's all. I know I'm not perfect by a long shot, but in that moment all I wanted to do was to be exactly what he needed. I never knew that marriage would be this hard. You know, when you think about marrying someone, you think about how much you love them and how good they make you feel (well at least I did). Now all I could think about was how much I hated him and how much he go on my damn nerves. That oxymoron "I love him but I hate him" fit my situation perfectly.

CHAPTER 4
Still Trying... But He's Stupid

Being home with Deon had been the most draining experience of my life. It was taking everything in me to serve and take care of him with a smile. All I kept thinking about were the vows that I had taken at that alter, "for better or for worse, through sickness and in health." I took a deep breath and placed the glass of orange juice on the tray next to the plate full with homemade Belgian waffles and scrambled eggs with cheese. I walked over to the kitchen table and grabbed the salt and pepper shakers, then placed them on the tray beside the bowl of shrimp and grits. Looking at the food made my stomach growl. I rolled my eyes remembering that I was dieting and all I would be having for breakfast would be two egg whites and a fruit smoothie.

After walking the breakfast up to our bedroom, I entered and greeted Deon with a smile and chipper voice.
"Good morning I made you breakfast."
"I'm not hungry."
"But I made your favorite shrimp and gr-"
"I said I'm not hungry," Deon said not lifting his eyes from the magazine in front of him.

I sat the tray down on the bed and stared at him in disbelief. Wow. What else did I have to do to try to lighten the mood in my own house? I had been walking on egg shells and kissing his butt for the past two weeks! What more did I have to do? I had taken off from work to stay home and wait on this man hand and foot and this is the thanks that I get? Was I missing something?
"For real Deon, don't take your attitude out on me. I didn't injure you. I'm trying to be here for you."
"You just don't get it Rose! You don't! This is my life! Football is all I know! If I don't get right after this, my career is over!"
"You're right. I don't know anything about football. But I do know that when one door closes another one will open. That's if you are open to another door. You sitting around moping and being a Grinch to everybody is not going to change anything.

Instead of being a whiner how about you start trying to come up with a plan B. I'm just saying."

This whole situation just reminded me of a life lesson that I had learned a long time ago. When it comes to life changes, women will roll with the punches. We will reinvent ourselves and flip all types of stuff sideways in order to make something happen. Men on the other hand... Let them have to step out of their comfort zone. Let something go wrong... They gon' whine and cry like a newborn baby.

"So what's this?" Deon asked, tossing the magazine at me.

I picked it up from the floor and looked at the cover. I knew that this was going to happen sooner or later. There it was, a picture of me walking out of a restaurant with Leandro. What I hadn't expected was for Deon to come at me like I was being untrue. This was unbelievable.

"What does it look like?" I asked him, tossing the magazine back at him.

"It looks like you're smiling harder with this gump than you do with me," Deon remarked.

"Oh is that so? I'm not about to sit here and entertain this nonsense. You know damn well Leandro is my client. There is nothing going on between us except business."

"Well can't business be done at your office, and not out in public eating together like yall are a couple?"

"Deon! You cannot be serious right now! You are acting like you have a reason not to trust me. Hello! I have been more than faithful to you! I have never cheated. Do I act like this to you, with your female assistant?"

"That's different."

"How? Please explain to me how different it is! I need to understand I really do! Look. I go out here and I work hard. I make it so you don't have to bear the whole load of providing for this family. So don't question anything that is work related. That's all it is. Work. You need to appreciate the fact that you have somebody that can go out here and make her own money."

"But don't forget who got you started," Deon remarked.

"DO WHAT?"
"I'm just saying. Now you all up on your high horse.. But you shouldn't forget the people that were there for you when you ain't have nothing."
"Excuse me? How can I forget about you? I sleep in the same bed with you at night. You are my husband! How many times have I thanked you for what you have done for me? How many times? But you know what? Hold on a second, I got something for you."

I walked into my closet and grabbed my Hermes bag. I fished through it and grabbed my checkbook and a pen then I came out of the closet and walked back over to Deon.
"Since being your devoted wife and the mother of your child isn't enough thanks for you... Since taking on the role of your child's mother even though Mocha tried to rip my family apart isn't enough for you… Since waiting on your grumpy ass hand and foot for two weeks hasn't been enough for you.. since nothing that I have done for you is enough to let you know that I appreciate you.. Then here you go," I said as I wrote a check payable to him.

I ripped the check from the book and sat it on the bed beside Deon. He picked it up.
"You ain't have to do all-"
"I don't even wanna hear it," I interrupted. "That's forty thousand. Exactly what you gave me to start the daycare center. But hold up. I got something else for you."

I walked back in my closet and pulled out my Louis Vuitton duffel bag. I unzipped it and grabbed ten bands, then tossed them on the bed.
"That's for all your pain and suffering," I said.
"Rosie you always gotta go to the extreme," Deon replied.
"Feel free to cash the check whenever you feel like it. You already know the money is gonna be there regardless.. My money is good, my checks don't do no bouncing."

I stepped back into my closet and put on a white chiffon blouse, then slipped on a black tailored pants suit. The thought of doing my makeup crossed my mind, but I wanted to get out of that house A.S.A.P. While slipping my red Manolo Blahniks on my feet, I grabbed my sunglasses and slid them on my face before I stepped out of the closet. Then I tossed the duffel bag in the closet and turned my back on Deon to leave. He sat in silence. I guess the cat had his tongue. Whatever. I was going back to work. I needed to get to my office, I had too much work to do to be fooling with his unappreciative ass. Violet had four more shoots to be finalized, and I had a deal to work out for Leandro. I hopped in my new Ferrari, grabbed my Ruby Woo out of the glove box, blotted a little on my lips, and sped off.

Once I pulled up, I felt a huge wave of relief. It was time to get back to work. The thought of making more money was exhilarating, and it most certainly took my mind off the tension that I was facing at home.

Lexi sat in the waiting area pretending to be busy at her desk. I didn't even bother to ask her what she was working on... I didn't want to put her on the spot. So I waved and kept it moving. I flicked on the light switch and stepped into my office. And what do you know? Right there, smack dab in the center of my desk sat a beautiful crystal vase filled with three dozen of pink and red roses. I smelled one of them and began to smile. It had been a while since Deon had sent flowers to my office. I figured that it was sort of a peace offering... Then I remembered... I wasn't even supposed to be in the office today. It was no way that Deon could have gotten those flowers there that quickly. I flipped over the tab and began to read. "Beautiful roses, for a beautiful rose... Thinking of you, but you will never guess who is doing the thinking... You will find out soon enough."

Perplexed was an understatement for what I was feeling. This definitely wasn't from Deon. I called Lexi into my office.
"Lexi, who brought these here?" I inquired.
"Oh yea. I don't know. I'm sorry. I was gonna call you and let you know they were here. They were delivered about thirty minutes before you got in. The florist's name is on the back of

the card."

"Oh OK," I replied.

My mind wandered trying to figure out who could have sent the roses to me. It was truly a nice gesture, but I knew for a fact that it wasn't from my husband. I took the card with the note on it and threw it in the trash. I decided that I didn't care who sent them, and I sat them on the window sill so they could get some sun.

I went on about my day, doing what I do best… Make money. It was something about being able to put food on my own table that I just couldn't get enough of. This gave me a sense of empowerment. My mind drifted back to the times when I didn't even have a house to call my own. My life was now the polar opposite. If only I could be happy across the board. My professional life and my personal life didn't match at all, and that was quite disturbing to me. Here I was with money in the bank, beautiful kids, multiple businesses, and people falling all over me when they met me… But I couldn't gain the attention and affection of my own husband. It broke my heart. All I wanted was for him to be happy for me. That's all.

"Mrs. Matteo, I think you need to look at Media Takeout," Lexi said with her face halfway through my doorway.

"Hell no. You know I don't look at nothing on that website. All they do is lie," I responded.

"I know… But Mrs. Matteo I really think you should look," Lexi said walking over to my desk with her cell phone in her hand.

She handed the phone to me, and I couldn't believe my eyes. There it was as clear as day, a picture of Violet walking hand in hand with that funny looking little boy. The caption read:

"Spotted rapper Young Bread in NYC...Looks like he has a new boo… Supermodel Violet… And they look super cute together!"

This girl had no common sense at all. Of all people, she wanted to be booed up with that fool. After all that I had told

her about him, she still had to go test the waters. For the life of me I just didn't see the appeal. Of all the wealthy and intelligent men that she had access to... She just had to get herself locked in with this twerp. Then to add insult to injury underneath the picture was another caption.
"Check them out in his new video, That's My Chic (click the link)"

I clicked the link and there she was in this stupid ass video, laying poolside in a bikini. I couldn't watch anymore. I handed the phone back to Lexi.
"Are you OK?" Lexi asked.

She knew how I felt about keeping Violet's career image squeaky clean. She understood how I felt without me saying a word.
"Just give me a few minutes," I said finally.
"OK."

Lexi left my office and I was left with my thoughts. I couldn't believe it. I was so pissed that I really wanted to pretend like I didn't see it. That way I could save myself an argument. But I couldn't bring myself to pretend. I had to call that stupid sister of mine.
"You just had to be dumb," I said when she answered the phone.
"Well damn, hello is how I thought you greet people when you call their phone," Violet responded.
"Whatever. I told you not to get involved with that ugly little boy. And you had to go and do the complete opposite."
"What are you talking about?"
"You know exactly what I'm talking about. Of all the dudes in the world... You gotta be with him?"
"Oh my goodness Rosie we're just friends."
"You're lying! That dude don't walk hand and hand with anybody unless he been in their drawers. So I already know you're screwing him. Violet you are putting yourself in a world of mess dealing with him. I'm telling you what I know," I warned her.
"Rosie I'm grown."

"Violet, you just turned twenty. Age alone doesn't make you grown."
"I don't need your permission to live my life," she replied.
"But you are my client. And you do need my permission to take a gig. But on top of being dumb, you went behind my back and did a video when I specifically told you not to! We did sign contracts. You do remember that right?"
"So what you gon' sue me? That would be really petty of you."
"Petty? Petty is sneaking behind my back with that clown, that's what's petty. If you were so real about yours then you would've told me you were doing it instead of me having to see it on Media Takeout."
"OK. Well it's nothing I can do about that now, what's done is done."
"You are so lucky you are in New York and not home because if you were I would come over there and slap the shit out of you!" I yelled.
"Rosie you're not my mother."

Everything in me wanted to hurt this girl... Physically and emotionally. But that wouldn't change anything. So I took a deep breath and calmed my attitude.
"Yeah I'm pretty sure that I'm aware of that. But since you know everything, I'm going to say this and then I'm going to leave it alone. Don't come crying to me when he breaks your heart," I said.
"He's not," Violet responded.
"OK. If you say so," I replied before hanging up.

I already saw where this situation was headed. Nowhere. I was hit with another life lesson. You can always see the danger of a situation when you're on the outside looking in, because being on the inside somehow makes you blind. It was nothing I could do but sit back and watch their so called relationship crash and burn.

The evening was starting to wind down and it was time for me to get on home to cook dinner. Since I was supposed to be home and not at work that day, I didn't have anything in the house already prepared for them to eat. So, I made my way to the grocery store. While I was on my way, I decided to call a truce with Deon. I was going to make a mouthwatering dinner for my family, put the kids to bed, and then I was going to make love to my husband. That was the plan for my evening. I walked the grocery store isles pondering on what to prepare. Then, it came to me. I would make some of his favorites. Steak, homemade baked macaroni and cheese, fresh collard greens, crab cakes, and banana pudding for dessert. This was sure to get him in a better mood.

After I finished my grocery shopping I went home and got in the kitchen. Miracle and Lil' Franko were already into their daily routine. They came home, did their homework, studied, and then took out their uniforms for school for the next day. Summer clung to my leg as I stood at the sink picking crab meat. I smiled as I prepared, and after Miracle was done taking out her uniform she came downstairs and helped me with dinner. I made sure that I taught her the basics of maintaining a home, and that included cooking. I had no plans of her depending on me for the rest of her life. I knew that one day she would grow up and have a family of her own, so she had to know how to cook. I went over to the trash can to throw away the tiny shell particles that I had picked from the crab meat and saw Deon's breakfast at the bottom. I felt an attitude brewing, but quickly simmered down. I said I was calling a truce, so that was what I was going to do.

"How do you know how much to put in there without measuring it?" Miracle asked as I scooped some mayonnaise into the crab cake mixture.

"I don't know, I guess it comes with experience. I hardly ever measure anything... I kind of always eyeball it. The only time I really measure is when I'm baking... Baking is science. You have to measure when you bake," I replied.

After dinner was ready I sent Miracle upstairs to tell Lil' Franko and Deon that it was time to eat. My son came downstairs, but there was no Deon.

"Mr. Deon said he's not eating," Miracle said.

"Well what is he doing?" I asked her.

"Um... He was on the phone," she answered back.

Nope. I wasn't going for it. I had slaved over a hot stove for the second time that day and here he was being crabby again. I wasn't having it. I made the kids' plates so that they could start eating. I knew they were hungry and I didn't know how long it was going to take to get Deon to come downstairs. So once I got them settled at the table, I marched upstairs to see what the problem was.

Sure enough as I approached our room, I could hear the bass from Deon's voice. I stood at the door, with my ear pressed against it.

"Well yeah. Or... You know I go to pain management so it won't be nothing for me to grab some blank prescriptions. He just leaves them out on the counter out in the open so I guess we can just do it that way," Deon said.

I couldn't believe what I was hearing. This fool had really lost his mind.

He began to speak again, "oh OK. I see what you're saying. Well I can just give you the money and you can go ahead and do what you do."

After all this man had accomplished in his life, he had reduced himself to this. He didn't even know if his injury would keep him out for good yet. What an idiot.

"Yea yo. I mean you know I got money but since I'm out from this injury I just need to keep it coming in. And I mean this ain't nothing that deep. I figure fucking with some pills ain't gon' be no big deal. I know we gon' have a whole lot though... But still that ain't that big of a deal. So yall can just meet up with me and I'll give yall the money and we can go from there," Deon said stupidly.

I had heard enough. It was time to break up this bullshit he was talking. I bust in the door.

"You just get dumber and dumber by the minute," I said.

"What?"

"I just stood on the other side of that door and listened to your whole conversation. What is wrong with you?"

"Hold up. Look... Yo let me call you back," Deon said into the phone before he ended the call. "Look Rose, I'm a man. Let me handle my business."

"First of all Deon, this ain't even you. How you gon' have a whole conversation like that on your personal phone? Then, how you know that ain't a set up? People know you play for the NFL! What makes you think a nigga won't get you somewhere, take your money then push your shit back and keep it moving?"

"Rose it ain't serious it ain't like I'm fucking with no dope or some other shit," he replied.

"So what Deon? I've seen people get killed for less! How you know they ain't working with the police? How you know they ain't the police? It's still illegal! Then what? You gon' go meet some dudes while you're on crutches? If something pop off how you gonna defend yourself?"

"Rose I got this, stop always putting your two cents in stuff that don't involve you."

"Deon this shit is a train wreck in progress. I could not honestly say that I love you and then let you go get involved in some stupid stuff like that. Come one now. Use your brain. And let me tell you something else. You have worked too hard to go to jail. Not only you. I HAVE WORKED TOO HARD TO GO TO JAIL. I will not have anything to do with anybody that is in that lifestyle. I just won't. So you better get a new phone, and whoever that was you were talking to you better lose their number. I'm telling you what I know."

"You don't' know everything!" Deon blurted out.

"Yea well I know enough," I said before I left the room.

   This made no sense at all. So you tear your ACL. Day after day you are mean and nasty to your wife. You don't return your agent's phone calls after he specifically says on your voice mail that he has an opportunity for you. And now you want to make plans to get wrapped up in an illegal prescription drug ring? I just couldn't with this guy. What next?

   I calmed myself down as much as I could as I walked back downstairs to the dining room. The kids were eating and running their mouths as usual. I made myself a small plate then

sat at the dinner table with my children. I ate in silence. Dinner had turned out extremely well. The steak was perfectly medium and seasoned. The crab cake was scrumptious. The macaroni and cheese was so creamy and the greens were my best yet. They reminded me so much of my Mama's greens that it was spooky. And to think, I had put all this love into this meal... Just for him to say he didn't want to eat. Did I have to write on my forehead "PAY ATTENTION TO ME" in order for him to get the message?
"Ma are you OK?" Lil' Franko asked me.
"Yeah I'm fine I'm just tired," I lied.

Well maybe I wasn't lying completely. I was tired, but not the tired that I portrayed. I was mentally tired. After dinner was finished, I offered dessert to the kids. Miracle decided that she was too stuffed and Summer followed everything that her big sister did so she didn't want any either. But my boy was always up for some banana pudding, so we sat at the table and ate out dessert together.
"So what was my father like?" he asked me out of the blue.

I almost choked on a banana. Lil Franko never asked me about their father. Neither did Miracle. Of course they knew that he was deceased, but honestly I hadn't even been the one to really explain that to them... Aunt Lucinda did that when I was still ripping and running the streets. So to have him just pop up and bring up the subject of his father was sort of awkward. I didn't really know what to say. I didn't want to be completely honest. I didn't want to tell him how much of a liar and a cheater his father was. That wouldn't do him any good. So I decided to go in the other direction with it.
"Well... You look just like him. He was funny... And he was really proud to be your dad. He was so happy when he found out that you were a boy... He was a cool guy," I said.
"Oh OK," Lil Franko continued on. "So he got killed right?"
"Yes."
"For what?"

Oh Lord. Now what was I supposed to say? It was no way that I could tell my son that his father was killed because he was having an affair with a married woman and her crazy husband found out. He was only thirteen. That was a bit much for a thirteen year old to digest.

"This crazy dude didn't like him," was how I managed to answer.

"Oh," Lil' Franko responded licking his spoon.

I knew that one day we would revisit this subject, but I was just glad to have gotten through it quickly this time. I always knew that one day I would have to explain to my children what happened to their father. That was part of the mental toll it took on me when he died. But it was nothing I could do about it, so that's just the way it was.

After Lil' Franko finished his dessert I wrapped up the leftovers from dinner, I took a nice hot shower. It seemed as though the tears which dropped from my eyes flowed at the same pace as the water that flowed from the shower head. I sat down in the tub with the shower still running and I closed my eyes.

"Lord I don't know what else to do. I feel like I am going to lose my mind Lord. Lord please give me a sign. I know I asked you before. Maybe I haven't been listening. But please… If I am not supposed to be in this marriage please show me. Please tell me. Please," I whispered.

After I finished my shower and dried out a bit, I put on some pajamas and camped out on the sofa in the living room with my favorite pink down comforter. The words of my prayer echoed in my head over and over until I fell asleep.

CHAPTER 5
A Storm Is Brewing

I stood at the sink cleaning greens so they would be ready for Aunt Lucy when she came up from VA. That would be one less thing that she would have to do. I was a little irritated because Deon's family decided that it would be too much for them to change their plans for Thanksgiving, but it was what it was. My cell phone rang and I wiped my hands on my apron before I looked to see who it was. I smiled when I saw Aunt Lucy's picture.

"Hey lady," I said cheerfully.

"Hey Rosie," she answered back.

"So when are you coming up? Did you decide on tonight or tomorrow morning?

"Um, I'm still not sure."

"Oh OK. That's cool. But look. I'm in here cleaning the greens for you now. I'm gonna peel the sweet potatoes for you once I finish this. I can't wait until Thanksgiving that food is gonna be so good," I chatted.

"Remember I told you I had to get my mammogram?" Aunt Lucinda asked off topic.

"Yup. You kept talking about them having to smash your boobs," I laughed.

"Well I got my results back."

"Oh OK. That's wassup. Oh! Before I forget, can you make sure you bring some cloves for the ham? I forgot them when I went to the grocery store," I went on.

"Rosie I have breast cancer."

I thought I heard her say she had breast cancer, but I couldn't be sure. I leaned up against the kitchen counter. .
"Huh?"

"I said I have breast cancer," Aunt Lucinda repeated.

"Are you for real?" I asked.

"I wouldn't play about something like that."

I didn't know what to say. How could this happen? We didn't have any history of breast cancer in my family, or at least I didn't know of any. And why would they tell her now at a

time like this… Right before the holidays?
"I didn't want to mess up your holiday; I just wanted to tell you. But don't tell anyone else. Not yet. I don't want everybody in my face about it. At least until I know all the answers to the questions that I know they're gonna be asking," she said.
"But what are you gonna do?" My voice cracked. "You know what? It's okay. Whatever you need I am here. You will have the best care. I promise."
"Rosie listen to me. I don't know what is going to happen. Only God knows. But I do know this. His will is going to be done regardless of what either one of us does. I will be OK. No matter which way it goes."

    Man. As if my life couldn't get any crazier, this comes. I didn't even want to think of the possibility of losing my aunt. She was the closest thing to a mother that I had. My eyes welled up with tears, and then they began to roll down my cheeks. I was at a loss for words.
"Rosie? Rosie are you still there?"
I cleared my throat, "yes."
"Listen to me. Don't worry about me. Get yourself together. Go ahead and finish doing what you were doing. Now that I think about it, I'm gonna come up first thing in the morning. OK?"
"Yea sure. That's cool. I'll see you then," I replied to Aunt Lucinda.

    This was a lot for me. I had never imagined that I would lose my mother in the way that I did… So when it happened, I nearly lost it. It took me years to digest the fact that she was gone. Now I had to face the reality that my aunt might be going too. I wanted to call Violet and tell her so bad, but I knew that she wouldn't be able to keep her mouth closed. She would either call Aunt Lucy right away and ask her, or she would be all in her face about it on Thanksgiving. So I couldn't tell her. I had to tell somebody. I just needed to get it off my chest. I thought about telling Deon, but quickly changed my mind. He had been more of my enemy than my friend these last few weeks, and you never share personal information with an enemy. Well maybe we weren't enemies... More like frenemies. So I picked my phone back up and called my best friend.

"Hello," she answered.

"Ro my Aunt has breast cancer," I sobbed into the phone.

"For real?" Rochelle was just as shocked as I was.

"Yes... Yes," I responded.

"Wow. Well... Don't worry. She's gonna be OK."

"What?"

"Rosie. She's a strong lady... With strong faith. She's gonna be fine. I feel it," Rochelle said.

"I'll call you back," I said before hanging up.

I don't know why I was so mad at Rochelle, but I was. She didn't know what was up ahead... But she made it her business to say that my Aunt was going to be OK. How did she know that? How could she be so sure? What if things didn't turn out that way? Then what? I finished the prep for Thanksgiving dinner then got myself ready for bed. Deon and I were in somewhat of a better place, so I had started sleeping in the same bed with him again. I thought about confiding in him again, but I quickly decided against it. We were on speaking terms (barely) but that hadn't changed the fact that all he seemed to care about was himself. My head hit the pillow and tears soon did follow.

The next morning I got up and started my day at about 6 a.m. I did my hour work out. After I cleaned myself up, I cleaned the turkey and prepped it so that on Thursday morning all I would have to do is pop it in the oven. Then I called Lexi to check on the progress of the Thanksgiving give away that I was sponsoring that evening. I had a busy day up ahead of me, and I was glad that I had gotten an early start. Miracle had the duty of looking after her brother and sister while I was at the event later on that evening. My kids' school was out since it was the day before Thanksgiving, and I had closed all my daycare centers that day as well. I went on about my morning like the busy bee that I was, but I couldn't help but drift to thoughts of Aunt Lucy. The "secret" had me feeling weighed down. I needed to talk to somebody in my family. So I called

Violet.

"Hey V," I said when she answered the phone.

"Hey. What's up? Are you ready for your event tonight?" she asked breathing heavily.

"Yup pretty much. Why do you sound like that? What are you doing?"

"I'm on the treadmill. Been on for almost an hour now."

"Oh OK. I did my work out already. Well look. I called you because I have to tell you something. But you can't say anything to anybody," I said.

"What? You're pregnant?"

"Oh my God no Violet. Why is it every time I tell anybody in this family that I have to tell them something, the first thing yall ask is am I pregnant? Have I not accomplished anything else in life besides having babies?"

"Well dag Rosie you went real deep," Violet giggled.

"Because yall always doing that and it's annoying," I answered back.

"Okay, okay, okay, I get it. So what do you want to tell me? Spill the tea please so I can get off this phone and turn the incline back up on this treadmill."

"If I tell you this V you have to promise that you are not going to say anything."

"I wish you would just go ahead and say it."

"Do you promise you won't' say anything?"

"What the hell is this a government secret?" Violet laughed

"V! Seriously! I'm not going to tell you if you can't promise to keep your big mouth shut," I asserted.

"Okay! I am sworn to secrecy. Now go ahead. This better be good too the way you're leaning on me this better be good."

      I took a deep breath. I could hear that little voice inside me saying, "Rose don't tell her," and I ran straight through the stop sign.

"Aunt Lucy has breast cancer," I said.

      There was a dead silence. I waited a few seconds for a response but got none.

"Hello?"

"Yeah I'm still here," Violet said in her driest voice.
"Did you hear what I said?" I quizzed.
"Yeah I heard you."

Then there was more silence. Once again I broke it.
"So just make sure you don't say anything to her about it, she didn't really want me to tell-"
"So why is this a secret? I'm not sure that I understand," Violet interrupted.
"Look, I don't know. You know how she is," I answered.
"And how long has she known this?"
"I'm not sure exactly how long but I'm thinking she found out recently because I remember her telling me that she was going for her mammogram like two weeks ago," I replied.
"Um," was Violet's response.
"Let's just give her some time to wrap her own mind around it before we start diving in," I suggested.
"So what stage is she in?" Violet asked.
"I'm not sure."
"Well what do you know?" Violet asked full of sarcasm.
"OK. So I see that you are upset so I'll give you some time to process it all," I replied.
"Yeah. Whatever. I'm wasting time on this phone with you let me call her myself."
"NO!" I screamed. "Why do you have so be so hard headed? I said she didn't want me to tell nobody so why would you go and call her? That's stupid!"
"So if you ain't want me to say nothing then why did you tell me? THAT'S STUPID!" she yelled back.
"Because I wanted to keep your retarded ass in the loop! See the next time I tell you something."
"All this family does is keep secrets. I swear... But whatever I'm not going to call her. Now I have to go. Oh and I'm bringing Anthony to Thanksgiving dinner."
"Who?"
"Anthony. Uuugghhh... Young Bread," Violet said before she hung up in my ear.

I wanted to call back and cuss her out, but I didn't have

the time and I was still working on trying to cut profane language out of my vocabulary. So I shook the whole conversation off and went on about my day. Besides, I could deal with her in person on Thanksgiving if need be. I got off the phone just in time, because Aunt Lucinda had arrived. She came right in and took over in the kitchen.

    I arrived at my event later on that evening bright eyed and bushy tailed. That was the way you had to be when people dished out money and time to your cause. I looked around and couldn't help but smile. We were going to be giving 2,000 families the ability to have a nice Thanksgiving meal. I was so proud but humbled at the same time (if that makes any sense). God had been good to me, so in turn I was giving back to the community. I had no reason to not be happy. Even though Deon had backed out of showing his face at the event at the last minute, I didn't care. I wasn't going to let anything spoil my night.

    Lexi had really done her thing putting the guest list together too. We had all types of celebrities there signing autographs. Athletes, rappers, singers, designers, radio personalities, reality T.V. stars, and models of color, including Violet.

    So the way things were set up was the venue was sectioned off into different areas. The area where you first walked in the door was where people came to pick up their Thanksgiving baskets. We also had appetizers and drinks for them so they could mingle amongst themselves once they received their baskets. All of our celebrity guests were situated in an area on the second floor of the venue, which was heavily guarded by security and decked out with lavish lounge furniture and a full spread of delicious goodies. Guests would alternate coming down onto the first level to greet some of the people who came to receive baskets. That's also where they signed autographs, took pictures, etc.

    OK. So I was on the second floor mingling with my guests. Violet had been avoiding me all night. Probably because she knew how close she had come to getting choked out for hanging up on me. But I was feeling too good to beef with her. I told yall I wasn't going to let anything spoil my night. Anyway, I looked over toward the staircase and there was Rochelle. I wasn't sure if she was even going to show up after I was so short with her on the phone the other night. It was a pleasant surprise to see that she still decided to come. She spotted me too and walked over to me.

"Before you say anything I already know you were acting stank because you were in distress so no need for an apology," Rochelle said.

"Well OK then," I laughed.

"Everything looks really good Rosie. You did a good job putting this together," Rochelle complimented.

"Thanks. But girl you know I've been super busy so I've had to trust Lexi to do a lot and she handled it well. I think I'm gonna have to give her a raise," I replied.

"Somebody is walking over here," Rochelle said.

"What?"

"Somebody is walking over here. He's smiling hard too," Rochelle whispered.

I felt a tap on my shoulder. I swallowed my champagne and turned to face him.

"Yes?"

He was bright. I mean like sunshine bright. Light skinned men were definitely played out.

"Hi. I just wanted to come and introduce myself. I finally get to meet the beautiful Mrs. Matteo in person," he said.

"Hello," I said extending my hand to shake his.

"Well I'm going to go on about my business, just wanted to say hello."

"And you are?" I asked.

Maybe I shouldn't have asked that. I mean his face broke down into so many levels that it wasn't even funny.

"You don't know who I am?" he asked.

"No, I can't say that I do," I remarked.

"I'm Billy Wanx."

"OK....."

"I play for the Red Sox," he said.
"And that's for what sport?" I teased. "Oh I'm sorry that's baseball right?"
"Yes. Baseball."

Boy had I crushed his spirit. Hahaha! I couldn't help it though. Deon played football, and I barely knew the names of his team mates so I definitely didn't know anything about baseball or the folk that played it. But he definitely was used to women drooling all over him. It was evident. His chest was stuck out so far that I thought it might pop the buttons on his shirt.

"Oh okay. Well thanks for coming out to support my event I appreciate it," I replied.
"So did you like the flowers that I sent you?" he asked.
"Flowers?"
"Yes. The roses I sent to your office."

My mind took me back to the day that I had received the flowers. So it was him who had sent them.
"They were nice. Thank you. But how do you know the address to my office?"
"I have my sources."
"Hmmm.... Well I'm pretty sure that your sources informed you that I'm married right?"
"Well that's public knowledge, but whatever. That has nothing to do with me. When I see something I want I go after it... I don't let anything get in my way," Bili Wanx replied with a snakelike grin.

This dude was a nut. There was no doubt in my mind. He must've encountered some truly desperate and weak women. Nothing about what he was saying was flattering to me. His arrogance was about as smelly as a skunk's ass.
"Well Mr. Wanx... I'm not sure what you are used to, but the only man I entertain is my husband. So I would appreciate if you wouldn't send me anything else," I said looking straight into his eyes.
"Oh. The hard to get role. I see. That's cool for now," he said still grinning.

I didn't even bother to respond. I turned around and walked away. Rochelle trailed behind me. She giggled so much I thought she was going to pee on herself.

"Damn he goes hard for what he wants," she continued to chuckle.

"Ain't nothing cute about a man on an imaginary high horse," I said rolling my eyes. "Even if I was single, a fat pink pig would have to mount up wings and fly like an angel before I would even let him smell me."

"Damn," Rochelle said shaking her head.

Maybe it was a good thing that Deon hadn't showed up that night. I really couldn't see that situation ending up well if he were there. Like the saying goes, everything happens for a reason right? Right. And can't nobody tell me any different.

I hopped on the elevator with Rochelle so we could check on how things were going with the basket giveaways downstairs. And if the elevator doors couldn't have opened at a better time... I swear to yall (I know I shouldn't swear Lord please forgive me) this is exactly how it happened... The doors slid open and there she was. ELAINA. Now what were the chances of this? I turned around to look at Rochelle and her mug was broke down, which signaled to me that she remembered exactly who she was. The last time that the three of us were in the same space wasn't too good. Rochelle was ready to dig in Elaina's ass when we went over to her house to drop off all the stuff for her kids for Christmas.

Well from the look on Elaina's face, she wasn't too happy to see us either. She rolled her eyes holding her basket in her arms. Now I could've been petty and snatched everything from her, because she had never even said thank you for the stuff I had gotten her kids for Christmas. But, being as though I'm not a petty bitch, I decided against it. I wasn't going to get any kind of blessings from being that way. So I stepped off the elevator and took the high road.

"Hi Elaina. How are you?" I asked.

Elaina didn't respond. She turned her back and attempted to walk away.

I wanted to slap that girl so bad. I really did. The nerve of this chic. What was her problem? Rochelle looked at me then took another sip from her glass.

"What you tryna do?" she asked me.

"Chill. I'm gonna go talk to her," I replied.

I put a slight pep in my step and caught up with Elaina. She was headed for the door. Once I was in arms reach, I grabbed her by her shoulder.

"What the fuck do you want?" she asked as she spun around to face me.

"First of all calm your tone."

"I'm grown don't tell me to calm my tone."

"You're right. You are grown. But, you are at *my* event and if you don't lower your tone I will have you escorted out."

The look on her face was priceless. Here she was again, getting help from little old me. The one she loved to hate.

"Look. What do you want?" Elaina asked in a modified tone.

"First I wanna ask how are the kids?"

"Like you really care."

"Elaina if I didn't care I wouldn't be asking. After you stopped bringing them to the daycare I stopped by your house to check on yall and your neighbor said that yall had moved," I replied.

"Yeah. We moved. But they're good."

"Oh OK Well that's good to know. Now... I just need to know what is your problem with me?"

"I don't have a problem with you," she lied.

"Come on Elaina let's be adults about this. The look on your face when those elevator doors opened up said it all. What have I done to you? Since the first time I saw you again at the daycare I have done nothing but try to help you. I'm not beefing with you anymore Elaina I told you that back then. So what is it? Are you still upset because I beat you up? If that's it, then I apologize. That's old. I'm not holding on to that and neither should you. It's no point in us being mad about a man who has been in the ground for a while now-"

"I'm glad it's easy for you to just say it's over with," Elaina interrupted.

"Because it is Elaina. Look. I already to you. I hold no grudge with you. Now you may hold one with me, but I don't see why. We are both grown women now with way more responsibility than we had back then. This little so called beef is really immature. But I'm not going to hold you up any longer," I dug in my purse and handed her my card. "My number is on here. I would love for Miracle and Lil' Franko to be able to get to know their sister. I'm not going to force it though. So if you want to, give me a call when you get a chance."

Elaina stuffed the card in her jeans pocket and walked away without saying a word. So at that point it was nothing I could do. I just hoped that one day she would reach out.

CHAPTER 6
A Not So Happy Holiday

Me, Violet, Deon, Aunt Lucinda, Rochelle, Miracle, Lil' Franko, Summer, and Baby Deon were all together for the holiday. Everyone sat at the dining room table with their plates in front of them ready to eat. Everything was piping hot and smelling so delicious. I couldn't wait to dig in. Aunt Lucinda had already said grace, but this year I wanted to do something a little different than what we unusually did at the table on Thanksgiving.

"OK, so before we feed our faces, I want everyone to say at least one thing that they are thankful for," I said.

"Aww man Ma this is that white people stuff I be seeing on TV. That's corny Ma I'm hungry," Lil' Franko whined.

Miracle laughed and I gave her the look. You know the look you give your kids to remind them that you will knock them the hell out. Miracle recognized the look and shut her mouth.

"Well would it be corny if God decided not to give us anything to eat because we don't let him know what we are thankful for?" I asked Lil' Franko.

"OK Ma I get it," he answered back.

"So, I'll start. I'm thankful for my family and I'm thankful for the success of all my businesses." I went on, "I'm thankful for God giving me another chance to get my life together."

"That's nice," Aunt Lucinda said with a smile.

I looked over at Violet. She hadn't said much all day and when she was quiet I knew it was because she had an attitude about something. But at this moment I couldn't be concerned with her little pissy attitude, it was time for her to say what she was thankful for.

"I'm thankful for honesty, and for people who don't keep secrets," Violet said staring at Aunt Lucinda.

I clenched my jaw then kicked Violet's ankle underneath the table. That girl had lost her mind. She rolled her eyes at me then took a sip from her glass. Rochelle looked across the table at me stretching her eyes wide open. She had caught the jab Violet threw just as well as I did. I looked over at Deon. It was his turn to say what he was thankful for but he was too busy nodding his heart out. I was so embarrassed. I knew that look. I used to have that look all the time. He was high. High as a giraffe's ass fooling around with that medicine. How in the world was I gonna be able to stay away from drugs when I had someone in my house reminding me of that old feeling? God that man was so selfish. He wasn't the man who I had grown to love. What happened to the old Deon who did anything to make me happy? It seemed as though he had run away from home never to return. My current situation sucked. MAJORLY. Even with all the things I was thankful for, I still needed some relief. Something had to give. My thoughts were abruptly interrupted.

"So why couldn't you tell me that you have cancer?" Violet asked taking a sip from her glass.

Aunt Lucinda looked over at me with the sharpest glare that I had ever seen. I wanted to slap Violet's face off. That girl couldn't hold water! Damn!

"I didn't want to ruin the holiday," Aunt Lucinda finally replied.

"What's cancer?" Summer asked.

"I'll talk to you about it later," I said to her in the calmest tone that I could.

"So when were you planning on telling everybody else? I mean is Rose the only person that gets to know stuff?"

"Now wait a minute V, you're getting out of line that's still your Aunt you need to show some respect," I said.

"Oh no Rose I can speak up for myself. Well first of all Violet I'm grown and I don't have to explain anything to you anybody," Aunt Lucinda snapped. "And now you know I have cancer so what difference does that make? I don't need this right now. I don't need anybody making this situation about them. I have too much to deal with and too many decisions to make. I don't need the foolishness."

Deon's eyes popped open and he re situated himself in his chair as if he had been alert the whole time. I took a deep breath tried to pull my family dinner back together.

"OK so Deon it's your turn to tell everybody what you're thankful for."

"You can skip me," he said.

"He ain't thankful for shit all he wanna do is pop pain pills all day," Violet blurted out.

"Says the girl who let half my team smash," Deon remarked.

Before I could even correct him, Violet picked up her glass and threw her wine in his face. I looked over at Summer. Her eyes were wide as saucers. Lil' Franko and Miracle looked like two deer in headlights. I couldn't believe what I was seeing. My beautiful family holiday was swirling down the drain right before my very eyes. This was bad. And it was only about to get worse.

"Stop it!" I screamed as I stood up and pulled Violet away.

"Why you grabbing me? He disrespected me!" Violet yelled.

"You can't talk trash to my husband at his own table!"

"But it's the truth Rosie you know it is. You already said he don't pay you no attention and all he does is pop them pills!"

Deon didn't say a word. He wiped the rest of the wine from his face with his napkin, grabbed his crutches, and then left the table. I grabbed Violet by her wrist and yanked her into the kitchen.

"What the hell is wrong with you girl?" I asked her.

"Ain't nothing wrong with me. What? I can't speak my mind?"

"Not if you are gonna be offending people and blurting out shit that was told to you in confidence! You get on my nerves with your stupid ass! Look you got me cussing like a sailor! I can't stand you sometimes!"

"I'm just stating facts. I just can't sit around and play like everything is perfect. That's not me. I'll leave that to you, that's what you like to do. That ain't my cup of tea though," Violet remarked.

I felt like my head was about to explode! That girl had a lot of nerve coming in my house stirring up a commotion like a pot of Maryland crab soup! It was taking everything in me not to knock her head clean off her shoulders... It really was. But if there was one thing I knew about Violet, it was this: she could dish it, but she never was the type to take it. So since I didn't feel like sweeping her teeth off of my kitchen floor, I had something for her.

"Oh? Facts? Facts you say? Well I like facts too. And the fact of the matter is you want to come in here acting like a little bitch because your broke ass hoe of boyfriend Baby Toast,-"

"His name is Young Bread," Violet interrupted me.

"I don't give a rat's ass what his name is. Little Buns, Broke Bastard whatever his name is... He ain't here. He ain't wanna be sitting up at no table with your family for no Thanksgiving dinner because let's face it... He ain't that in to you," I went on. "All he wanna do is screw you when he feel like it and keep your nose wide open so he can use you up then kick your ass to the curb like he does everybody else. Both you and I know he's probably somewhere humping on some hood rat when he claiming he's at the studio. So before you come in my house trying to set off landmines in my comfort zone, you need to take an assessment of what's going on in your own life."

"You think you better than me? You ain't better than me! Just cuz you married?"

"Girl please you sounding like you 16 again cut it out. Look I have guests to entertain. So since you wanna act like a spoiled brat go stand in the corner and take a time out," I said making my way back toward the dining room.

    I was all ready to apologize to Aunt Lucinda for the circus that had erupted at my dinner table.

"Where's Aunt Lucy?" I asked looking at her empty seat.

"She left," Rochelle responded.

"She left?"

"Yup she left," Miracle said stuffing a piece of ham into her mouth.

"So why didn't anybody come and get me?"

"Rose ain't nobody wanna come in that kitchen in between you and Violet going back and forth. She told me to tell you that

she would call you once she got back to Virginia to let you know she made it back safely," Rochelle replied.
"But if one of yall would've came and told me I could've stopped her from leaving!" I yelled.
"She didn't want to be stopped Rose. It seems like she just wants to be in her own space right now. Let her have her space," Rochelle said.

Before I could give her a piece of my mind about telling me how to deal with my aunt, out comes Violet from the kitchen. I saw red.
"Get out of my house you fucking trouble maker!"
"Look at Ms. Perfect yall! Look at Ms. Church this and Jesus that! You so fake. Christians don't cuss like that. You a fake bitch," Violet spewed.

Rochelle got up from her seat. She already saw where this was headed. I stood behind my chair silently contemplating my next move.
"Come on let's go upstairs yall," she said as she gathered Miracle, Lil' Franko, Baby Deon, and Summer up from the table.

Violet must've realized that she was in danger too, because now she was slipping on her shoes and gathering her purse. She tried to push past me to get to the front door once she was finished, but at this point the kids were out of sight and we had some unfinished business.
"Oh so you think you gon bump into me?"

I grabbed Violet by her neck and forced her against the wall.
"I told you before to stop playing with me! I will kill you in here!" I screamed as Violet struggled to breathe.
"Rose get off that girl neck like that you gon' kill her!" I heard from behind me.
"Rochelle don't touch me. This bitch wanna act a fool in my house, I'mma treat her like a fool in my house."

Rochelle grabbed a hold of my right hand and peeled back my thumb. Lucky for Violet this loosened my grip and she fell to the floor.

"I said said don't touch me!" I screamed at Rochelle.
"Girl you ready to go to jail over an argument with your sister? You trippin'," Rochelle said.
"Whatever," I responded as I grabbed Violet by her ponytail.
"Get off of me! Rochelle call the police!" Violet pleaded.
"Rochelle don't touch me, I'm not doing nothing to her, I'm just putting her out since she didn't know how to do it on her own," I replied.

Rochelle stood there staring at me with a look of disgust. I knew that she thought I was crazy, but I didn't care. As threw Violet out of my front door, I had one more thing to say.
"And find somebody else to manage your bum ass! I don't need you!"

I slammed the front door and returned to my dining room. I was getting too old to be doing all that. I was tired. I sat down at the table, trying to assess what had just happened in my own head. My daze was broken by Rochelle's voice.
"You know you can't do that right?" she asked.
"What?"
"You can't just tell her you're not managing her no more. Yall have paperwork binding yall together."
"Whatever I don't care," I replied.
"Yall two make me sick. For real. I cry every night missing my brothers. And all yall wanna do is fight and disrespect each other. It's sickening," Rochelle said as she grabbed her purse.
"So what I'm supposed to just let her talk shit to me in my own house?" I asked.
"It's a way to do things Rose. You know that. You're better than that. I mean really. But who am I to tell you?"
"Here you go with the sarcasm," I uttered.
"Call it what you want. Yall are sisters but yall always fighting like some ratchet girls in the street. I can't with yall. I just can't. I'm gone. I'll holla at you later I guess," Rochelle said before she headed toward the front door.

I didn't say a word. She was entitled to her opinion... *I guess*... But she was only on the outside looking in. Nobody really understood the relationship that Violet and I had. Hell, most of the time I didn't even understand it. I took a deep breath and decided to wrap up this disaster of an evening. I called the kids back downstairs to finish their dinner while I cleaned up the kitchen and put all the left overs away. Deon didn't come back for his dinner. He stayed upstairs in the room which I had expected him to do anyway. What a holiday.

CHAPTER 7
Checks

"Rosie I'm sorry," Violet said accompanied by her puppy dog eyes.

I tapped my pen on my desk. How many times had Violet apologized for disrespecting me? Hmmmm.... More times than I had fingers. This girl had ruined my Thanksgiving and now here she was in my office trying to come back to the winner's circle. Some nerve she had.

"So what makes this different than any other time Violet? Please let me know how? You don't know what to say out of your mouth. And it always causes a problem," I replied.

"And you have a problem with your hands Rosie. So it seems as though we both have problems."

I took a deep breath. This girl was really wearing my patience thin. You can not apologize to someone and then turn it around on them. That's not how apologies work. You are supposed to come humble and sincere and if the person you are apologizing to decides to give an apology back, then that's a different story.

"Violet... You never cease to amaze me. You come waltzing your little behind in here like you want to mend things, yet you still can't shut your mouth. But whatever. I see now how I have to treat you. I'm going to treat you like the model that I am managing, since I know the only reason you even attempted to apologize is because you know New York Fashion Week is coming up. And I'm not going to sit here and act like I don't like checks either. So with that being said, I will email you the schedule. That email will also contain your flight and hotel accommodations. Enjoy the rest of your day," I said before I hit the speaker button on my desk phone.

"So have you talked to Aunt Lucy?" Violet asked.

I knew this girl had a mouth on her but I didn't know that she was hard of hearing. I spoke into the phone.

"Lexi I'm ready for my 11:45." I let the button go, then looked at Violet. "This meeting is over, enjoy the rest of your day."

Violet's eyes welled up with tears. I stared straight

through her until she got up and left. I had no time for the foolishness. I was tired of all the craziness with that girl. At this point, it was all about the checks.

Anyway, it was time for my 11:45 appointment. This was something I was very excited about. Nervous, but still excited. This was a chance for me to break into a whole new genre of checks. REALITY T.V.

"Good afternoon Mrs. Matteo," Matt said as he shook my hand.

"Good afternoon. Please sit down," I replied as I directed him to the seat on the opposite side of my desk.

Matt was one of the producers at VH1. He and I had been conversing over the past month or so about the possibility of doing a reality show. He cut straight to the chase.

"So... Have you made a decision on the show?"

"I'm leaning towards it... I'm just kind of on the fence about a few things," I responded.

"Like what?" Matt asked.

"Every time I even peek at a reality show there is somebody fighting. Always. I really don't want to have to do that in order for people to watch. I don't want my family or my business to be seen in that type of negative light."

I laughed in my head. A flashback of me throwing Violet out of my house on Thanksgiving popped in my head. That was the type of stuff I didn't want the world to see.

"I understand your concerns," Matt went on. "Most of the time that has a lot to do with editing. He juiciest scenes are put back to back to make the show seem more exciting so to speak. But it's not like people are fighting 24/7. It's not like that."

"Is that right?" I asked.

"Yes. But I totally understand if you still need more time to think things over. Let me ask you a question though Mrs. Matteo... How does your husband feel about the possibility of having a show?"

"I haven't talked to him about it yet honestly. I've been really busy and my schedule has been so tight that I haven't had time to sit down with him about it," I lied.

Well it wasn't a total lie. I hadn't talked to Deon about it, but not because of my busy schedule. It was because half the time I couldn't stand him and the other half he was too busy popping those damn pills. I couldn't telly Mr. Producer Matt that though. I had to keep that squeaky clean image.

"Oh OK Well once you guys talk it over just give me a call and I can sit down with the both of you and the rest of the production team," Matt said.

"OK That sounds like a plan to me. Thank you for meeting with me, I appreciate the opportunity," I said as I reached across the desk and shook Matt's hand once more.

The rest of my day was pretty hectic. I had to finalize Leandro's travel accommodations for his underwear shoot for Calvin Klein. Then I had to go sign off on an incident report from the daycare because the fax machine at my office had been down that day. After that I had to go get Baby Deon from school early so that I could get him to his 2:30 doctor's appointment. Once his appointment was over, I had to go pick up Summer from Deon's mother, then pick up Franko and Miracle from cheer leading and football practice. By the time I was done all that running around, I was exhausted. Once I got in the house, I immediately kicked off my pumps and collapsed on the sofa. Finally I could get some rest. As soon as I started to drift off, here came Miracle.

"Ma, you still making lasagne tonight... Right?"

Well I guess rest was out of the question when it came to me. I guess I didn't deserve it. Or maybe that's what everyone else in my house thought. I didn't say a word. I got up from the sofa,then walked into the kitchen and put on my apron. Back to work I went. I browned the grown beef with Summer clinging to my right leg. I layered the lasagne in the backing dish while Lil' Franko read his essay aloud that he had been writing for his English class. I put the lasagne in the oven, then made a salad in between signing Baby Deon's permission slip for the aquarium, and writing a check for Lil Franko's new football uniform.

I sat down at the island in the kitchen and my cell

phone rang. It was Deon. I answered.
"Hello?"
"Where you at?" he asked.
"I'm home."
"Home?"
"Yes. Home. Cooking dinner. Whats going on?" I asked.
"You are supposed to be here twenty minutes ago to pick me up from therapy," Deon snapped.
"Oh my goodness I forgot!"
    I immediately jumped up from my chair and grabbed the car keys from the counter.
"Yea you always forget something. Well I'm here waiting," Deon said without waiting for a response from me.
    I didn't have time to call him back and chew him out for hanging up in my ear, so instead I just headed for the door.
"Miracle!" I yelled.
"Yes Ma?"
"Look after everybody while I go get Deon. In fifteen minutes, take the lasagne out of the oven and sit it on top of the stove. Make sure you use the oven mitts!
    I cleared the front door and jumped into my car. I anticipated the attitude I was going to receive once Deon got in the car. And I was right.
"You only remember the stuff that's important to you," he said as soon as he sat in the passenger seat.
"Well I'm here now so you can cut the attitude," I answered back.
"But you're late."
"But I had an extremely busy day."
"Well why don't you take my advice and hire an assistant?"
"I have an assistant," I said knowing where the conversation was headed.
"You know exactly what I'm talking about. Not for work, somebody who can help you with stuff at home," Deon responded.
"No I can handle it."
"Evidently you can't."

"Well how about you try to do what I do every day," I shot back.

"Why won't you just get somebody to help you around the house?" Deon asked clearly agitated.

"You know why," I squeezed through my clenched teeth.

"Why?" Deon continued to pry.

"BECAUSE I DON'T TRUST YOU THAT'S WHY!" I blurted out.

The truth was, Deon cheating with Michelle still cut like a knife. And I would be damned if I had any other woman in my house doing anything for my family but ME. Call me crazy but I don't care.

"I made a mistake Rose. I can't take it back."

"Yeah I know that. But I'm still not opening my house up for another woman to be up in there like she owns the place. I'll pass."

Deon didn't say another word. And neither did I. I can't say that I was upset that the rest of the ride home was silent either. I really didn't want to hear anything else Deon had to say. Not his nagging, not his complaining, and I for damn sure didn't want to hear anymore of his stupid ass suggestions. All I wanted to do was get home, serve my dinner, clean my kitchen, wash my body, and get in my bed.

By the time everyone had eaten dinner and I had cleaned the kitchen, I wanted to pass out. I went up to the bedroom and started to prepare for my shower.

"Dinner was really good," Deon said as I undressed.

"Thanks," I responded.

That was kind of puzzling. Sure we had been speaking, kind of... But I hadn't received a compliment from him in I don't know how long. It's a terrible thing when you feel strange about your own husband complimenting you. Anyway, I went on about my business. I took my shower, brushed my teeth, and got in bed. I felt like I was sinking into the mattress. Nothing else could've made me feel better at that point. I was in paradise.

I've realized that people really take for granted all the

things that mothers do on a daily basis. We wear a lot of hats. At times, it can be too many. And when we get a little tired or irritated by having so much responsibility, the world sometimes has a way of making us feel like we are wrong for feeling that way. I mean, HELLO! WE ARE STILL HUMAN!!!

OK. Enough of that rant, back to the story. So I was laying in bed minding my business drifting off to dreamland and the next thing I know, I feel a hand on my butt. Well not *a hand*, it was *Deon's hand.*
"Is it a reason you have your hand on my behind?" I asked him.
"Do I need a reason to touch my wife?" he chuckled.

Oh Lord the man laughed. Something had to be going on.
"I didn't even know that you still acknowledged that," I said.
"Acknowledged what?"
"That I'm your wife."

There was an immediate silence. I had struck a nerve. But the elephant in the room had to be addressed. I wasn't about to sit there and pretend that he hadn't been present in our marriage for quite some time. He was there, but not really.
"Of course I do," he said finally.
"Well I can't tell," I replied with my back still turned to him.
"Why are you talking to me with your back to me?"
"Because I didn't even know we were about to have a conversation. I thought I was going to get in bed and go to sleep in silence like I've been doing."
"Turn around and talk to me please," Deon requested.

The tone of his voice sent a chill through me. Not a bad chill, but a good one. You know the type of chill that only the person that you love with everything in you can give you. So I did what he asked.
"So what do you want to talk about?" I asked once I situated myself.
"I love you," he said.

I took a deep breath. Something had to be wrong.
"Why are you saying that?"
"Because I do Rose. I know I haven't been the best lately. And I

know it's no excuse, but this injury has really taken a toll on me."

"Deon let's be real. You've been acting like an ass way before you tore your ACL. Seriously."

"You're right. I'm not even going to lie... I just want my wife back. The one that was always there when I needed her," Deon responded.

"Are you serious? Deon... As much as I work I still make sure that you and the kids are taken care of. I'm not going to stop working... That's just not going to happen. And with the type of work that I do, I have to travel too. But if you want to go with me, you can. If you want to stop by the office sometimes, you are more than welcome to. I don't extend the offer because every time we are around each other it just seems tense and you give off this vibe that you don't want to be bothered. I need you to stop nagging me all the time about work. I'm doing this for us. Not just me. All I'm trying to do is go out here and get these checks. That's all I'm after when I'm a work. Not another man, not another family. Just checks."

"Are you sure you ain't out there scouting for something new?" Deon asked.

"No. I don't want anybody but you Deon. I don't know how many times I'm gonna have to tell you this. You are my husband and I have no desire for anybody but you."

Deon kissed me and I felt like I was floating in mid air. I gathered enough strength to come back down to earth.

"Now lets talk about some real stuff... The pills Deon... The pills have to go."

"You know I need them for my pain," Deon whined.

"Listen to me Deon. I see where this is headed. You need to talk to your doctor about weening you off that stuff. Seriously. Opiates ain't nothing but heroin in a pill. Do you get what I'm saying? You have to stop," I commanded.

"Yes. I understand I'll get better. I promise. Now can I please have my wife?"

Why did it take this long to have this conversation? Why was I walking on egg shells in my own home for the past four months? I just couldn't understand it. But none of that mattered now because I was wrinkling up my Ralph Lauren sheets with the man that I shared a last name with. Tore up leg and all. Yup. I let him have me alright.

The next morning I woke up feeling like a million bucks. I had swung from the chandelier all night and I wasn't the least bit worried about the crazy schedule that I had to tackle that day. Everything was all gravy. There's another life lesson that I learned a long time ago. A night of awesome sex can change your whole perspective on life. Ha!

As I went on about my day, I couldn't help but to drift back to the conversation that Deon and I had the night before. Maybe I hadn't been showing Deon enough attention. So I decided to do something special for him. Maybe this could sprinkle some happy glitter into our marriage. So I got on the phone and booked a photo shoot with Lenour Madrid, one of the most sought after photographers in New York. Yea, this was going to be good.

Next, a location... Something exotic... Somewhere warm and Sunny... Somewhere that I could wear my bikini and entice my man for our entire stay. St. Lucia. Yes that would be perfect. So I booked a six day seven night stay at Jade Mountain resort. I had it all planned out in my head. I was going to do a super sexy shoot with Lenour, and give the pictures to Deon once I got him to our vacation destination... And then we were going to just enjoy each other, with no kids, no work, no nothing. Just us two. It was going to be perfect. And to think, he was complaining about me working so much. How else could I do things like this for him if I wasn't out here getting these checks?

CHAPTER 8
Photo shoot

I sat down on the bed in my hotel with a nagging nervousness in my gut. In exactly two hours I had to be at my photo shoot. What was I thinking when I came up with this bright idea? But I was already in New York, so there was no turning back now. I wanted to do something nice for my husband, something that I knew he would like. Before the awkward shift between us had started, he would always ask me to send him selfies throughout the day when both of us were working. So I knew he would love to have some professional pictures of me.

Deon must've been thinking about me too, because in the midst of my thoughts my phone rang.
"Hey baby," I answered.
"Hey," Deon answered back in a dry tone.

I knew that tone. That tone meant he was unhappy about something. I dreaded that tone.
"What's wrong?" I asked.
"What do you think?"
"I don't feel like guessing, so why don't you just tell me?"
"Don't you think I get tired of sitting home while you go fly here and fly there?"
"I don't know.. Maybe you do. But who's holding you hostage Deon? I asked you did you want to come with me, but you said no. So what do you want me to do? Get up and do something! I can always make arrangements for the kids! Put them crutches to use!"

God this man was sucking the life out of me. No matter what I did, it was always a complaint. Not even three days ago we had a talked about why I worked so hard and that me working didn't mean that I was trying to disconnect from him. And here he was again with the bull shit. Damn! I'm cussing again. Anyway, back to the story.
"It's always something with you. It's always business. Everything is business." He paused for a second then went back in."So what you a model now?" Deon asked full of salt.

"You know what Deon? I'm going to hang up this phone before I cuss your stupid ass out," I said before disconnecting the call.

What in the world was wrong with this man? Here I was trying to do something special for him. I was trying to surprise him and he was making it extremely hard for me. I was ready to just call everything off. He didn't deserve all of this. I decided to call Rochelle to get some sound advice.

"Ro I'm getting so tired of him and all his complaining and whining I don't know what to do!" I screamed into the phone.

"Okay girl just calm down," Rochelle snickered. "This too shall pass. He just wants you home so you can rock his world that's all."

"I'm not even joking Rochelle he is just doing too much! I'm out here literally scared to death, stomach in knots about to do a damn photo shoot to surprise his cry baby ass and all he can do is call and nag!"

"Well Rose he doesn't know that you are out there trying to put together a surprise for him so cut the man some slack. He just misses you that's all."

"Well if that's the case then he should've came up here with me!"

"But ain't you glad he didn't? How were you going to keep it surprise if he was right there with you?"

"Rochelle I already had it planned out I told him that I was doing a shoot for a perfume campaign that I was teaming up with Violet on," I informed her.

"Oh... Well... Still. Just chill girl. As soon as yall get home yall will be good. Go ahead and kill that shoot. Calm yourself down and call me when you're done," Rochelle replied.

It's good to have a friend that can talk you off the ledge every now and again. It would've been hard to hide what I was doing from Deon if he was there with me. But his behavior was still childish, and that was something that we still needed to work on. He had to know that I was going to have my own life and my own career, whether he like it or not. Period. That's how it was going to be. But I decided to put those issues on that back burner at the particular moment, and focus on the matter at hand. I slipped on my floral print monokini and went and sat in the sauna that was located on the first floor of the hotel, adjacent to the pool. I wasn't sure if it was going to make a difference or not, but I wanted to look as slim as I possibly could. Maybe I could shed a few ounces of water weight, and maybe not... But it was worth a try.

    I spent about thirty minutes in the sauna (even though the sign said not to exceed twenty) and then I went back up to my room. It was time to go on over to Mr. Madrid's studio and face the music... Well in this case... The camera.

    Once I go there, I had to go straight to hair and makeup. I don't understand how Violet does it as much as she does. Having people pull all on your hair and put layers and layers of make up on your face. It wouldn't be so bad if the process didn't take so long. In the words of the greatest rapper alive Mr. Jay-Z himself, "I got no patience, and I hate waitin'." Sitting for long periods of time really irked my soul, so this process was no walk in the park for me. Now don't get me wrong... When I got done, my face and hair looked good. No great... But still, I could've gone without the long process that it came along with.

    Finally it was time to start the actual shoot. My stomach was still doing back flips. Maybe it was because I had arranged for this to be an implied nude shoot, one where you are basically naked but you find some type of way to cover your private parts. After a few test shots to make sure the lighting was right, it was showtime.

    Mr. Madrid's assistant helped me out of my robe and there I was. EXPOSED. I hadn't had any man see my body other than Deon in years. I thought that maybe they could see my heart beating through my chest, because it could feel the vibration of it all over my body. I took a deep breath and positioned myself on my knees showing my profile with one of my arms covering my breasts. Then I turned my head back just a little, with my eyes directed behind me. I parted my lips just a tad bit, and then there was a flash. That was the first image. I looked at Mr. Madrid and he cracked a slight smile. I

forgot how much of a trip he was to look at. He was a tall thin white guy with long blonde hair that hung down a little past his butt and he always wore all black with a matching leather fanny pack. Every single time Violet had shot with him he always had on black from head to toe. He had the same look that day. He wore gold rings on every finger, reminiscent of Mr. T, and he had a hoop nose ring. And when I say he was white, HE WAS WHITE. Like baking soda white. With blue eyes. You got the picture in your head? Right.
"And this is your first time doing this?" he asked.
"Yes. I mean I've watched Violet... But you know the type of stuff she does... High fashion... So I'm just doing what I think looks good," I said.
"OK, well lets keep going," he replied.
    After taking a few more shots, I started to get nervous all over again. I wasn't getting any type of feedback from Lenour and it had me a little worried.
"Can I see?" I asked him already knowing better.
    Photographers do not like pausing a shoot so you can look at your images. I learned this from being on set with Violet. But I was feeling so self conscious. I couldn't help it. He looked up from the camera.
"I usually don't interrupt my work to-"
"I know. I just wanna make sure I'm looking right," I said. "But if you don't wanna let me look I understand."
    He came closer to me and leaned in so I could look into the gallery.
"You have a beautiful body," Mr. Madrid said.
"It's OK I guess," I replied.
"OK? You are gorgeous."
    I didn't reply. I wasn't gonna debate with him about my appearance. Truth is, after I had Summer I had put on some weight, and I had been struggling with it. I would lose fifteen pounds, then gain back ten...Then lose ten and gain back fifteen. It had been rough. I couldn't even believe that I was doing the photo shoot in the first place. I was just trying to add a little spice to my marriage. To kind of wake Deon up to what

he still had... Even though my view of my own self was kind of screwy.

"Have you ever thought about modeling?" Mr. Madrid asked.

"Oh noooo," I replied.

"Wow. That was a strong no," he chuckled.

"Because I haven't. I'm no model. I leave that to my sister."

"OK. I see. But with your body type I think I have an opportunity that could be good for you," he remarked.

"Mr. Madrid, I'm flattered that you think I could model but that's really not my thing."

"Just hear me out. A business associate of mine has a line of lingerie-"

"Lingerie? Oh no I can't."

"Rose just listen to me. As I was saying. He has a line of lingerie for women with curvier body types. His stuff isn't for size twos and fours. Well anyway, he's looking for a model for his relaunch of the line. I think you would be perfect."

Now would you look at that... Here I was in New York, doing something for my own pleasure... And a new opportunity for business just dropped in my lap. I smiled on the inside. Then my heart rate picked up speed. The thought of having pictures of myself with lingerie on for the world to see took my mind back to my stripping days. I had worked so hard to get away from that. I wanted to be seen as a business woman, not as a sexual object.

"Look. I'm not asking you to make a decision right this minute. Take some time to think on it. Once you come to a decision just give me a call and we can move on from there," Mr. Madrid said.

"OK," was all I could manage to say.

"Alright. Well lets get back to this shoot hot Mama! Flip that hair back!" Mr. Madrid said with the camera up to his face.

I arched my back and flipped my hair and our session resumed.

CHAPTER 9
The Last Straw

It was Friday and it was time for me to get back to Baltimore. Deon was back to not speaking to me again, and I was way too exhausted to care. I didn't have the strength to argue. I didn't have any fight in me at that point in time. None. When I got back from New York, all I wanted to do was get some sleep. Violet was still trying to get back in my good graces, so she agreed to pick the kids up from school and take them out for the evening.

I stepped through my front door and felt a wave of relief. As tense as my home life had become all over again, it still felt good to be home. I didn't even have enough power in my legs to make it up the stairs. I dropped my luggage in the middle of the living room floor and collapsed onto the sofa. I needed a nap.

I woke up from my nap in a panic. I knew I had to do something! I was going to be late picking Deon up from physical therapy. I had made arrangements with his mother for her to drop him off and I would pick him up since I would be back from New York in time to do so. Lord knows he was already a grouch, but when I was even a couple minutes to pick him up it was the end of the world to him. I went in the bathroom and brushed my teeth, then I grabbed my phone and car keys before I rushed out of the door. I looked at my phone and saw that there were twelve missed calls from Rochelle. "Damn, what she wanna talk about?" I thought to myself as I sat the phone in my lap.

I didn't have time to call her back though, I had to get to Deon. So I buckled my seat belt and put the car in drive. Just as I was pulling out of the garage, Rochelle was calling again. I put the phone on speaker.
"Hey Ro wassup?"
"Hey. What are you doing? Why you ain't answer my calls?"
"I was taking a nap. I had like and two hours free today, and I was so tired.. So I didn't even try to do anything, I just took a nap. But I'm on my way to pick Deon up from physical

therapy."

"Come past here before you get him," Rochelle said.

"Ro I can't I'm already late," I explained.

"Rosie it's really important."

"Well tell me now while I'm on the phone."

"No, I need to tell you in person," she said.

Something wasn't right, I could feel it in my spirit and I could tell by the tone of her voice. This wasn't her usual, "I got the juicy gossip" tone. This was way bigger than that.

"Shit Ro, he is gonna be fussing. But ard, I'll be there in like ten minutes," I said.

"OK," she said.

I pressed my foot a little harder on the gas pedal and my phone began to ring again. It was Deon. I already knew what he was going to say so I cut him off.

"I know I'm late I overslept I'm on my way bye."

My mind raced as I tried to figure out what was going on with Rochelle. I couldn't draw up anything though. I pulled up to her house and parked any ole' kind of way. I got out of the car and looked at my car's crooked position. I shook my head and kept it moving. Before I got all the way to the door Rochelle was already opening it.

"Damn what you was in the window?" I asked.

"Yea." she responded.

"Ard wassup? I said crossing the threshold.

"Sit down," Rochelle said closing the front door.

"Ro I don't have time I told you I'm running late."

"Rosie, please sit down at the table."

I looked at her face and I couldn't read her expression at all. What in the world was going on with my best friend? I sat down to appease her.

"OK.. Now wassup?"

"Well.. Um.. I.. Well... Uh..-"

"Girl what the hell is going on?" I interrupted.

"Well.. Guess who called me?" she asked.

"I don' feel like guessing just tell me."

"Guess!"

I tried to think of somebody that we wouldn't expect to call her. Then it popped in my mind.... Her old guy from the Red Fish. Yall know, my old faggy boyfriend's faggy friend.
"I don't know! Who? Nico?"
"Girl hell no! He better not fix his mouth to call my phone."
"Ard then well who?"
"Deon."
"Deon who?"
"Your Deon."

I paused for a second.
"So what did he call you for?" I asked.
"Um... He was trying to get me to come over there."
"OK.. I'm confused... For what?"
"Rosie... He was trying to get me *to come over there.*"

My heart sank. I couldn't believe that this was happening to me. How could he embarrass me like this. I could take a lot of things, but being embarrassed was an emotion that I just couldn't stomach.
"Oh yea? OK then," I said heading for the door.

Rochelle reached the door before I did and blocked me in.
"Hold on Rosie. Let me tell you what happened before you leave," she said to me.

I didn't respond, I just looked at her.
"Well, the other day when I was over your house and you left to take him to physical therapy, like ten minutes before you got back, I got a blocked call. So I answered it and it was a dude on there basically saying that he wanted me and I kept asking him who he was, but he wouldn't say who he was. He said he couldn't tell me because his wife would kill both of us. So I told him wasn't nobody going to touch me. I wound up hanging up since he wouldn't tell me who he was. So yesterday, the blocked number called back and I answered again. This time, I kinda recognized his voice. So I just kept asking who he was and finally he told me," Rochelle explained.
"And he said It was Deon?" I asked.
"Yea. So I told him don't call no more or I'm gonna tell you.

Then he hung up. So this morning he called back from your house phone-"

"Ard. Move," I said to her.

"Don't go doing nothing stupid, Rochelle said.

"How do that sound? You just told me that my husband is trying to sleep with you and then you want to tell me not to do nothing stupid? Let me out!"

Rochelle moved away from the door and I stormed out. I got in my car and grabbed my phone. I went to Deon's number and sent the call.

"Where you at?" he asked.

"So you tryna fuck Rochelle?" I asked.

"What?"

"You heard what I said! How dare you? How fucking dare you? I'm on my way over there!"

"She lying!" Deon lied.

"Well if she is lying, then when I come pick you up you're gonna go over her house with me and tell her to her her face that she is lying!" I screamed before I hung up.

At that moment I don't know what I was feeling.... I was mad, and I was hurt, but most of all I felt betrayed. But the most important life lesson that I had stopped thinking about was to never put anything past anybody. Sure, Deon had cheated before, but never in a million years did I think that he would try his hand with someone as close to me as Rochelle. I raced down the highway to get to Deon. I already was mapping out in my mind how I was going to kick him in his leg and tear his ACL all over again. Once I got outside of the physical therapy office, I called his phone but he didn't answer. Then I texted him that I was outside, and still no response. By this time I was highly agitated. I got out of the car, slammed the door, then stomped into the office.

"I'm here to pick up Deon Matteo," I barked at the receptionist.

"Mr. Matteo left about fifteen minutes ago," she stated rolling her eyes.

"Bitch don't roll your eyes at me because the way I'm feeling you will get the shit smacked out of you for no reason at all," I said before storming out.

    The whole ride home I called Deon back to back and I didn't get any answer. He was really cruising for a bruising. So I devised a new plan. I was gonna go home and change into my ass whipping gear, then I was gonna hunt him down like the dog that he was. I couldn't wait to get my hands on him because when I did, it wasn't gonna be nothing nice. So, I pulled up to my house and to my surprise what did I see? This cripple nigga and LeVelle's sneaky ass carrying Deon's stuff out to his car! I threw the car in park and jumped out. I started my war path in the garage.

"Oh so she was lying right? Oh OK," I said as I grabbed the rake.

"I don't even want to fuss so I'm leaving," Deon copped out.

    I swung the rake at his head and he ducked, still holding onto one of his crutches. I didn't care that I missed, because I had other plans anyway. I took the rake and started to beat the hood of his black Maybach. I dragged it back and forth trying to make as many scratches as I possibly could. Deon somehow got the rake away from me, after he suffered two blows to the head.

"Chill out girl damn! You don't have to act so crazy!" he yelled at me.

"Oh I'm acting crazy? Imma show your lying sneaky no good ass crazy!" I yelled.

    I ran in the house and looked around. There were a few bags with some of Deon's clothes and shoes thrown in them. I made a mental note and ran into the kitchen. I opened the cabinet over top of the stove and grabbed a bottle of vegetable oil, and a bottle of olive oil. I unscrewed the tops and tossed them on the floor. I saw Deon coming toward me and LeVelle was behind him. I ran around the kitchen island and flung the oil all over his bags of clothes.

"LeVelle man grab her!" Deon yelled, hopping on his one crutch.

"Man I ain't touching her! She ain't fucking me up!" LeVelle yelled back.

"Yea you better not touch me because I will bust your head in this fucking house and then I will fuck your bougie ass wife up if she even think she gon' have something to say about it," I said as I threw the empty bottles at Deon's head. One connected.
"Ahhh! You bitch!"
"Oh I'm a bitch?" I asked.
    I ran over to the stove and grabbed the grate from off of the right front burner and went ham on Deon. He was doing his best to block the hits, but it was too difficult for him to block them all. He finally got it out of my hand and threw it on the floor. While trying to back away from me, Deon slipped in some oil and fell. Bingo. This was the perfect opportunity for me to stomp that damn leg. I took the first kick and it landed. Deon hollered in pain. I went in for a second, but LeVelle grabbed me by the back of my shirt and yanked me back.
"Didn't I tell you not to fucking touch me?" I screamed.
"I'm not gon' stand here and let you stomp on that man's leg you taking it too far," LeVelle stated in his own defense.
"I don' give a fuck how you feel! Mind your fucking business," I said before I grabbed the salt shaker off the counter and hummed it at his face. It hit him smack dab in the center of his for head.
"Man I'm getting out of here before I really put my hands on her," LeVelle said rubbing his forehead.
    Just as Deon tried to get on his feet, I heard voices in the house. Violet was walking in with the kids. She had taken them out to the mall and to dinner. They walked through the family room and that's when all hell really broke loose.
"What is going on in here?" Violet asked, looking at the mess.
"This clown gotta get the fuck up outta my house," I said to her.
"Ma... what's wrong?" Miracle asked.
"Go upstairs yall," Violet cut in.
"But what's wrong Ma are you OK?" Miracle continued to pry.
"I said go upstairs! Take them with you," Violet said placing Summer's hand in Miracle's hand.

The kids scurried upstairs and I went in.

"You sorry pill popping muscle head bitch. After all I have put up with. After I stood by you with your crazy ass baby mothers and you cheating on me in my house with Michelle. And now this?"

"You ain't perfect! What you forgot where I met you?" Deon screamed.

I knew for sure that I would be going to jail that night. I felt myself getting hot all over. Now it was war. I ran to the hall closet and grabbed my baseball bat. Deon must've known what I was going to the closet to get because he was already heading for the door. I caught up with him and swung the bat as hard as I could. It made a loud thud as it connected with his back. Deon screamed in pain. I chased him back outside into the driveway and he jumped in the car. I guess he thought he was safe. Not. I swung hard. The bat smashed the front windshield.

"Rosie no!" Violet screamed from behind me.

"Get out the car!" I yelled. "Get out of the car! You wanna call yourself bringing up old shit? Get out the car and watch me fuck you up!"

Finally LeVelle jumped out of the car and ran to his. He got in and locked the doors.

"V go get me a knife!" I screamed at Violet.

"A knife? Rosie what are you going to do?" Violet asked.

"Just go get it!"

Violet went in the house and I stood in front of Deon's car. He rolled down the window.

"Rosie get out the way! Just let me leave!" he yelled.

"Naw bitch you got so much mouth get out the car!" I screamed back.

Violet came back outside with the smallest knife that we had in the house. I wanted to cuss her ass out but I gave her a pass. I snatched it from her hand then put it in Deon's front driver's side tire. Then I followed up with the other three.

"Rose you are a crazy bitch!" Deon yelled.

"Now you really ain't going nowhere. Let's see you drive off on rims."

I went back in the house and grabbed as many of the clothes that Deon had in the living room as I could. As I was coming out of the house, Violet was running up to the door.
"Rosie somebody called the police," Violet said out of breath.
"Damn. I didn't close the security gate," I thought.
    Violet picked up the knife and dropped it inside the rosebush. I glanced out to the end of the driveway and sure 'nough there was a police car. Oh well. At this point I was so pissed that I didn't care. I walked to the end of the driveway to meet them.
"Hi mam. What seems to be the problem here? We got a call about some type of disturbance," the officer said.
    I threw the clothes that were in my arms on the ground. Before I could say anything Deon spoke up.
"Officer I just want to leave that's all," he said getting out of the car finally.
"Oh now you want to get out of the car," I said.
    Deon grabbed his crutch from the ground and hopped over to where we were. The officer looked over at Deon's car.
"Mam did you do that to his vehicle?"
"Yes I did," I replied.
"Listen officer. I don't want to press charges. She didn't touch me. I will take care of my car. I just want to be able to get my things and leave," Deon said.
"OK. That sounds fair," the officer responded.
"I bet it does. But him trying to cheat on me with my best friend isn't fair at all," I said.
"Well Mam unfortunately there's nothing I can do about that. I need you to sit out here while I escort him in so he can get his things. Then he's gonna leave."
    I didn't even bother to respond. I got in my car and I broke down. Violet stood out in the driveway. She didn't get in the car with me. She just looked. I looked out the window and watched Deon limp to Le'Velle's car. He got in and the pulled off with the police officer right behind them. I couldn't take it anymore. At this point I knew for sure that there would be no going back. Deon had messed up too many times. I had tried

my best to hold this thing together, but it was time to hang it up. My marriage had run its course.

I went into the kitchen and grabbed the Crown Royal apple from the bar. I poured a shot and sat down on the wooden stool at the island.

"Are you OK?" Violet asked me.

"No. I can't even lie. I'm not," I responded.

"Well maybe yall can work this out," Violet said.

I took the shot straight down then poured myself another. I wanted to be mad at Violet, but I couldn't. She was young and naive. She didn't have a clue about marriage. She was still under the impression that married folk are supposed to work it out no matter what. That was so far from the case.

"No V. This can not be worked out. He tried to sleep with my best friend. I can never trust him again. I wouldn't even take myself through that torture. The marriage is over. I just can't do it anymore," I said before I took the second shot, then poured a third.

I could hear Summer whining. I wanted to go upstairs and get her, but I just didn't have any strength left.

"V please go tend to her. I can't do it right now. I need a few minutes to get myself together."

"Yea. She's probably sleepy. I'll get all of them to take showers and get them ready for bed."

I swallowed the third shot without giving Violet a response. She went upstairs and I was left by myself with my thoughts and my liquor. What a combination. This is what my marriage had come to. My life and my happy home had transformed into one that wasn't happy at all. Was I not good enough? I mean, I felt like I was! But obviously Deon didn't. There were a lot of things he could've done to me out of spite or because of whatever he was going through. But this... This had to be the lowest. This was the most disrespectful thing that he could do. I was so disappointed in him. I was hurt. I felt used. I felt taken advantage of. I felt inadequate. I felt empty. I felt confused. And I was so fucking angry. How could somebody who claimed to love me keep taking me through so many changes? And then the memories of walking in and seeing him laid up on my sofa with Michelle flooded my head. I was overcome with sadness. I had been a fool. I shouldn't have taken him back. Now look at me... I was crying my eyes out trying to drown my pain in Crown Royal. How could he do this to me?

Now how was I going to come back from this? My marriage had failed. And now I was going to have to settle into the life of a divorced woman. I didn't have a choice. It was no way we were going to be able to get past this. It was no way I was going to be able to trust him again. I would never be able to even handle him being in the same room as Rochelle. My heart ached. But what was crazy was that I still had a piece of my heart that was trying to figure out how we could work this out. But I had to let this life lesson sink in... I had to go with my mind on this one, I couldn't follow my heart. You can't help who you love and emotions have the tendency to complicate things. Your heart is going to lead you purely on emotion... But your mind... Your mind is going to lead you by reminding you of your common sense. I had to leave my heart out of it this time. It was going to be hard, but it's what I had to do.

CHAPTER 10
Papi Knows Best

  I sat at the dining room table drinking my cup of coffee, black with no sugar. I was still trying to dry out from the day before. My head felt like somebody had hit me with a rock in a sock a few times, and my eyes were literally sore from all the crying. Violet offered to take all the kids with her for the weekend and I gladly took her up on it. I needed some time to figure some things out. I needed to be responsibility free for a couple days.

  Earlier that morning while I was in the midst of one of my crying spells, I got a phone call from Juan just checking on me. In case yall forgot, Juan is my father who I just met a little over two years ago. Well anyway, he heard what he referred to as the pain in my voice and decided that he wanted to come over and talk. I agreed. It would be nice to actually talk to him face to face, without anyone else being around. The other couple times that I had been around him, it had been with other family around... I guess the both of us weren't really ready to have that real alone time. But today would be the day. I took another sip of my coffee and as I placed my mug back on the coaster, the doorbell rang. I got up to answer the door.

"Hey Juan," I said as my father entered the front door.

"Hey Rose," he answered back taking off his hat.

"How are you?" I asked.

"I'm good I can't complain. You?"

"I'm alive," I responded.

  Juan looked around. I could tell he was admiring my place, it was much bigger than his house. He looked at the sofa as if he wanted to sit down, but wanted me to give him my approval first.

"You can sit down," I said to him.

"Gracias," he responded as he took his seat.

"Now look Juan, I don't know no Spanish like that so take it easy on me," I joked.

  He laughed. Good my attempt to break the ice had worked. Thank God. I didn't like tension at all and I didn't want

my father to feel uncomfortable in my presence.
"So what's going on? What's bothering you? When I called earlier you sounded pretty broken up."

Even though I didn't want *him* to feel uncomfortable... I did. I didn't really know him well enough to be going into detail about how my marriage was in shambles. I took a deep breath. The light bulb went off. I didn't want to be sitting in awkward silence. so I guessed now was the time to ask him all the things that I had been wanting to know.
"Um... I don't really want to talk about that...So... I guess what I really want to know is... Where were you all this time? I mean... Why weren't you around?" I asked.

Juan took a deep breath. I could tell that he had been dreading this conversation. I understood how he felt though, because as bad as I wanted answers I was still kind of scared to get them.
"Your mother and I kind of ended things on a sour note," he answered back.
"So what happened between you and my mother? Like why... Well why weren't you-"
"Why wasn't I there when you were born? Or during your childhood? Well it's kind of a difficult story. I mean if you really want to know I'll tell you."
"Yes I want to know. I need to know," I said.

My father was silent for a little while. Long enough for me to know that what he was about to tell me wasn't going to be good. Finally, he broke his silence.
"Well... I was with Lucinda during the time you were conceived."

Did he just say what I thought he just said? No he didn't. No this man didn't. He didn't really know me so he didn't know how much I despised disloyalty. This was too much. So even though I knew exactly what he was saying, I decided to ask the question anyway.
"Lucinda who? Like my Aunt Lucinda?"

Juan swallowed hard then looked me straight in my eyes. I already knew what his answer was going to be. Man this was gonna hurt.

"Yes, your Aunt Lucinda," he said.

As if my life couldn't get any screwier. As if my history couldn't be more soap opera-ish. What in the world? I never looked at my aunt in that light... Like NEVER. Not my bible toting, church every time the doors were open, scripture quoting Aunt Lucinda! This was too unreal!

"So let me get this right. You were sleeping with my mother and my aunt at the same time?" I probed.

"Well not at the *same* time... But-"

"You get what I'm saying. That's some real snake shit," I replied.

My God... I had grown up and went after nothing but dogs. Dog, after dog, after dog... Not even knowing that I came from the dog-est of all dogs. Its funny how life works. It always has a way of showing you how messed up it can be. Somewhere deep inside me I had hoped that when I finally met my father he would have some deep story about how he had searched far and wide for me, and that he was a stand up guy and my mother was just bitter and kept me away from him. But honestly, I understood why she didn't want any parts of him. I totally flipped out when I found out about Franko and Elaina. I don't know what I would have done if it had been my sister. Damn.

"I know I was wrong," Juan said interrupting my thoughts. "But it's nothing I can do to change what happened. I wish I could, but I know I can't. I do apologize for not being there for you though. When I reached out and your mother gave me a hard time, I should've pursued you more. I always wondered where you were."

I was speechless. And for anyone who knows me, that's a very rare occurrence. I wanted to know, and now I knew. Now what? Should I punch him in his throat and kick him out my house? Do I call him everything but a child of God? I was torn! I was in the midst of some serious spiritual warfare you

hear me? Every other minute I was thinking of ways to kill Deon... Then here came my own father telling me of how he betrayed my mother, so naturally I wanted to kill him too. And Aunt Lucinda! That info made me want to drive all the way to Virginia just so I could slap her face... But what would that solve? And what would that make me? I had to stop letting others control me by angering me, whether it was intentional or not. So instead of getting physical, I decided to get as much understanding of the situation as I could. I exhaled.
"So how did my mother find out?"
"I don't remember the exact details, but from what I remember Lucinda and Viola got in an argument about something... About what.. I don't remember... And Lucinda kinda like blurted it out," Juan replied.

My mind raced back to the day that Aunt Lucinda told me that Leon wasn't my father. She specifically told me that she didn't know who my father was. Well we all see now that was a lie. I said it before and I'll say it again. EVERYBODY HAS SKELETONS IN THIER CLOSET.
"And when she found out she was pissed and told you to stay away from her and her child," I suggested.
"Basically."
"Wow."
"And she kind of made herself scarce. Stopped answering my calls. Then changed her number. She stopped going to the salon so I couldn't see her there-"
"Salon?" I asked puzzled.
"Si. I mean yes. I met your mother and Lucinda at my sister's salon. I used to do all the repairs there."

Yup. I was officially done with this conversation. I had heard enough. Finding out that my mother and aunt were in a love triangle with the handy man at the Dominican salon they went to, when they should've been in there getting blow outs and carrying their asses home was really enough for me.
"OK that's enough right now I don't wanna hear anymore. I don't wanna get any madder than I already am," I blurted out.
"OK I understand," he said.

So in crept the awkward silence that I had tried so desperately to avoid. This is why we hadn't been alone. We both knew that we didn't have enough in common to hold a half decent conversation. We barely had a father/daughter relationship. Hell, we barely knew each other for real.
"So, where are your kids?" Juan asked finally.
"They're gone with my sister for the weekend," I answered back.
"Oh that's nice. Now you and your husband can have the house to yourselves for a little while."

Now why did he have to go there? Tears welled up in my eyes. I blinked them away. But I couldn't think up a lie to tell Juan. And he picked right up on the bad energy.
"Uh Oh... What's wrong?" he quizzed me.
"Nothing... I mean I don't wanna talk about it," I said.
"It seems like you need somebody to talk to. I'm here for you Rose. I'm hear to listen. We all need a listening ear sometimes."
"I want a divorce."

It's like the words spilled out of my mouth. It hurt me so bad to say it aloud... Hearing those words come out of my own mouth made it more real.
"A divorce? What's going on?"
"He cheated. Well he tried to cheat. With my best friend. And he cheated before... With the nanny. It's just time to let it go. But I don't know if I'm doing the right thing. I don't want to be the cause of my family being torn apart," I said.
"Rose listen. I know I haven't been around... But I'm usually a good judge of character. I'm not just saying this because you are my daughter either. You are smart. You are ambitious. You are loving and very giving of yourself. You deserve better than that. You walking away from someone who doesn't deserve you and who doesn't know how to treat you like the queen you are is does not mean that you broke your family up. He broke your family up when he decided to cross you... More than once. I'm a man and I'm telling you from a man's point of view. I've done a lot of wrong, so I know what I'm talking

about. Leave him alone. Let him be. If you keep taking him back, then he's going to keep on doing it. He can only do what you let him do. He's not ready for what you have to offer. You can stand on your own two feet. You are la jefa... That means you are the boss... Everything in this house flows through you. Keep building your empire. A worthy man will come along and be everything that you need him to be... Trust me."

    I looked at Juan... I mean... My father. I tried to blink the tears back again but it was no use. All my life this is what I had wanted. Approval from my father. Out of all those years that I had been abused by who I thought was my father, I had never gotten his approval. And after I had found out that he wasn't even my father, that made it even more tough. All I wanted was my daddy. And now I had him. My papi. Juan Sanchez.

"Why are you crying?" he asked getting up from his seat.

    I put my head down in shame. I wasn't sure what I was ashamed of though. Maybe it was because the first time I had a real conversation with my father I broke down and cried. Or maybe it was because it had taken him to tell me what I was worth for me to actually realize it. Or maybe it was because ever since I found out that he was my father I had a secret hatred for him for not being there, and in my mind I saw a monster... When in all actuality, he wasn't that bad. Sure he had made some mistakes, but he seemed to have learned from them. Either way, I was an emotional wreck.

    My father wrapped his arms around me and I felt safe. I felt secure. I felt exactly how a girl is supposed to feel when she is up under her daddy. It felt good. I took a deep breath so that I could try to get the words out.

"Thank you," I said.

"For what?"

"For being here. I needed you and I didn't even know it."

    He squeezed me even tighter and I cried even harder. What a release. It's like I felt all the stress evaporate into thin air. Its amazing what a good cry can do to you.

"Well since you have some time to yourself, how about you

come over to the house? Adelina is making enchiladas," my father said releasing me from his embrace.
"OK, that sounds good," I said wiping the remainder of my tears.

So, fast forward through the car ride over there. Everything was all nice and light. I was in the kitchen with my step mother minding my business trying to get the inside scoop on these enchiladas that she was making. Then in comes my brother (by Juan and Sina) with a cut off netted yellow shirt and tangerine shorts looking like he stole is outfit from a Ken doll. I looked him up and down waiting for him to speak. The first time I met him I spoke first and her barely spoke back so I wasn't going to make the same mistake twice. He walked right past me like I was invisible and stuck his fingers in the pot of shredded pork and pulled some out. After eating it he was getting ready to exit the kitchen, but I wasn't having it. It was time to put his brown ass in his place.
"So that's what you do? Walk in a room and don't speak?" I asked him.
"What?" he asked knowing damn well he heard what I said.
"You heard what I said. What's your problem? You come in here like you own the place, stick your hand in this woman's pot without even washing it, and you didn't even speak to either one of us. Is it a problem?"

Adaelina looked at me like I was crazy. I could tell that Manuel ran things around there, and nobody dared to speak up when it came to him. Well, I ain't live there, and it wasn't one thing that I could even think about finding scary on him so he was going to hear what I had to say. If he didn't like it, oh well.
"I don't even know you really so its really no reason for me to speak to you honestly," Manuel said swinging his ponytail over his shoulder. "I mean all you are to me is my father's bastard child that broke up the family."
"Well what you mad at me for? At least he was around for you! You wanna walk around with your ass on your back because your parents ain't together? Well woopdie fucking do! That's a tiny issue compared to all the shit I went through growing up!

So you can miss me with all that petty shit! Either you're gonna accept me as your sister or you're not it's as simple as that! No, you know what? You don't even have to accept me, but you will respect me."

"Or what?" he probed with his hands on his hips.

"Or you gon' catch this ass whipping from a real woman. What you wish you were," I snapped.

Before I could even get up in his personal space like I wanted to Juan was in the kitchen.

"What's going on in here?" he asked me.

"Your son is rude and disrespectful and I think he wants me to put my hands around his neck," I said.

"Papa' decirle a este vagabundo que ir a casa!" Manuel screamed.

"Say it in English faggy!" I said charging toward him.

Juan jumped in front of Manuel, which made me furious. I should've known he would take his side. He had been around him all his life. Adaelina stood at the stove in silence. She seemed to know when to stay out of things that weren't any of her business.

"Stop it Rose. I don't have this in my house," Juan said to me.

"But he's the one—"

"Just stop it. Please stop," Juan said before he turned to Manuel. "Si no puede ser respetuoso entonces usted tiene que salir!"

And that's when the shit really hit the fan. Manuel knocked everything off of the kitchen counter including the toaster and the electric can opener. Juan slapped Manuel in the face. Manuel started crying and zapping out in Spanish. Then Juan got loud on Manuel. I can't lie, I was kind of getting a kick out of the whole scene. I looked over at Adaelina. She had turned the pot off, and was sitting in the chair, still saying nothing. In the middle of Juan laying him out in Spanish, my mind began to wander. Manuel said that I was the bastard child that broke up the family. Exactly what did he mean by that?

"Can I speak with you for a minute outside?" I asked Juan as Manuel stormed out.

"Sure. Give me a minute," he said as he went out of the back door.

I picked up the mess from the floor. Adaelina went back to the stove. There was something about her that I couldn't put my finger on.

"Are you OK?" I asked her.

"Yes. I'm fine," she said.

One thing about us women, no matter who we are... No matter the shape, weight, age, height, or race... We all have that one line in common. I'M FINE. I wasn't going to pick her apart about it, even though I knew she was lying. So I decided to go join my father on the back porch. When I got out there he was staring off into the distance smoking a cigarette. That whole little episode had bothered him. I felt kind of bad about it. If I hadn't said anything to Manuel, this could have been avoided. There's another life lesson. Pick and choose your battles wisely. A lot of times it's not even worth the hassle or the headache. And there are always casualties, ALWAYS.

"Hey," I said.

"Hey," he replied exhaling smoke.

"I'm sorry about all that. I should've just ignored him."

"Manuel needs an attitude adjustment. He's mad with the world. So don't be sorry. About time somebody checked him."

Juan took a deep pull from his cigarette. I wanted so badly to ask him how he was dealing with having a son who was openly gay and flaming, but I decided that right then wasn't the time. What I did know was that he hadn't turned his back on him, and that was commendable.

"So... Manuel said that I broke up the family?"

"Manuel is a hateful person."

"Yeah. I get that. But why did he say that?" I asked.

"It's kind of a messy story Rose," Juan replied.

"I'm listening," I said.

Juan took a deep breath. So did I.

"So I told you your mother went to my sister's salon. Well my wife at the time worked there too... And that's who used to do your mother and Lucinda's hair. When I found out that Lucinda

had told your mother about me and her, I told her I didn't want to deal with her anymore. I guess Lucinda wanted to get back at me, so she told my wife, well my ex wife about the whole affair. She told her everything. She told her that I got Viola pregnant. And she told her that I had been sleeping with her too. So she divorced me. We had a nasty divorce. She took everything. She told Manuel everything. So he knows about your mother. It doesn't give him the right to be ignorant about it though. It's the past and nobody can change that. Things happen. Nobody is perfect. Things fall apart in order to come together. I lost my first marriage because I couldn't be faithful, I didn't have any kind of self control. But I learned from that. I've never cheated on Adaelina. I'm just grateful she gave me a chance after seeing how everything went down."
"Went down where?" I asked.
"At the salon. She worked there too," Juan said before he dropped his cigarette butt and stomped it.

    Now that was a mouthful. My father used to be a hoe. I wanted to be mad, as usual. But how could I? I was in no position to judge. I used to be a hoe too. I guess the saying is right. The apple don't fall too far from the tree.

CHAPTER 11
I Still Got It

So since I was technically single, I thought it would be cool to go mingle on the single scene. I was still avoiding Rochelle, so I was flying solo that night. I sat in the V.I.P. section of the club with my body guard, Timmy. I only went out with him when I went to clubs... That's where people tended to act like they ain't have no sense with all the liquid courage they be drinking.

Even with all the loud music and drunk people I was bored. I was bored and I was sleepy. I was bored, sleepy, and annoyed. You never realize how annoying drunk people are until you are no longer an annoying drunk person. Ha! That's crazy ain't it? I wanted to go home. This definitely wasn't my cup of tea. And to think, once upon a time I worked in an even more raunchy environment than this! I was ready to go. I could have a better time at home in my bed with some popcorn and cranberry juice. So I whispered to Timmy that I was ready and he got me out of there seamlessly. My driver was waiting outside just like he was supposed to. I loved when people executed their jobs to a tee. Just as the door was opened for me to get in, I heard my name.
"Rose!"

I turned around to see who was calling me and I recognized his face. It was Brent, one of Deon's teammates.
"Don't come any closer sir," Timmy said with his hand on his gun.
"No, Timmy. Chill. Let me talk to him for a second," I said.
"OK I'll go over there with you."
"NO. Let *me* go talk to him. I'll be fine."

Timmy didn't respond he just kept his hand on his weapon. I walked over to Brent.
"Hey wassup?"
"Nothing much. Just wanted to say hello. I couldn't get to you in the club," Brent smiled.
""You were in there? I didn't even see you," I replied.
"Yea I know. You were too busy in your phone. And when you

did look up, you looked like you were miserable."
"That's because I was," I laughed.
"Not really your scene huh?" Brent asked.
"Nah. Not anymore."
"So you headed home?" he continued to pry.
"Yup. Gonna cuddle up with my kids and chill in my pajamas," I answered back.
"OK Well I don't want to hold you up. I just wanted to know if you would be interested in letting me take you out sometime... You know... Show you a good time."

    Well wasn't he something? It didn't take him long to warm up now did it?
"I can't do that, you're his friend. That wouldn't be right."
"Well technically, I wanted you first."
"What do you mean by that?" I asked.
"Look the first night we came to the club, I told Deon that I was looking for you. I was the one who had heard about you being the best dancer there. But once we got there, he straight asked for you. I wanted you. I wanted to take you out of there from the first moment I saw you," Brent said.

    My mind was all over the place. True I was mad at Deon, but there were certain lines that you just shouldn't cross.
"But like I said, you're his friend. I can't do that."
"I'm not his friend. I play on the same team as him.. But I'm not his friend. I'm not friends with dudes that don't know how to treat their wives."

    Wow. Even he knew that Deon was a certified dog. Damn. So how did I miss it?
"Oh look at you! You got all kinds of palm trees growing all around you!" I exclaimed.
"What?" Brent asked.
"Meaning you're throwing shade. You know palm trees... They give shade.. Look never mind. Just.. This ain't right. I'm flattered but I can't," I said before I walked away from him toward my car.
"That walk is mean Miss," he called out to me.
"I know," I said as I got in.

I settled in my seat as comfortably as I could before I pulled out my compact mirror. I was blushing. Hard. Brent was a really handsome guy. He had a nice buff build. He wore a regular haircut... And the waves in his hair could make you feel like you were about to capsize... His skin tone reminded me of gingerbread, and he was covered in tattoos. I WANTED HIM. But I couldn't have him. Such a disappointment. But hey. I didn't need the distraction anyway. I needed to focus on my career, and I needed to focus on getting out of this marriage as quickly as possible. It would be nice to be bad for a change though. An alert from my phone interrupted my thoughts. I had a voice mail. It was Rochelle.

"Call me when you can," she said.

I wanted to call her, I really did. But the embarrassment of the whole thing just wouldn't let me. How could I face her after my husband had been trying his hand? I just didn't know what to do. I had never felt so unsure about myself in my life. I would call her eventually. No tonight thought. I wasn't ready to have that uncomfortable conversation. And that was my right. So I got home, took a nice hot shower and called it a night.

My days went on as usual, work, kids, Deon begging to come back... Kids, work, Deon begging to come back. Work, kids, a little traveling here and there, and of course Deon begging to come back... I wasn't interested though. He had me and didn't know how to treat me when he did, so now he had lost me. Why does it take for people to lose what they had to realize that it was good? Why do you have to give chance, after chance, after chance to make someone do right? Why do you have to *make* them do right? Why can't they just do it on their own? BUT... There was no sense in throwing myself a pity party. I was alive and I was healthy and so were my children. Plus I had booming businesses and plenty of money in the bank. It just wasn't my time to have a man I guess. And that wasn't the worst thing in the world. I had definitely been through worse. Somebody would snatch me up and treat me right. I still had it. Just had to wait on he right one to recognize it.

One Friday morning, while at the office I got a Skype from a very familiar face. It was Paul. Let me fill you in on him. He was a very busy and financially stable guy. He had his hand in a little bit of everything. Real estate, an urban clothing line, a comedy show line up that toured the United States, a trucking business, and Loyalty Records which was his record label. He always reached out to me when he needed models for his clothing line campaigns, so we were very well acquainted and had a pretty tight business relationship. He never tried to haggle me when it came time for him to sign on the dotted line for Violet, and I respected that. In this business, men always tried to give women a hard time... But not him, he respected my hustle just as much as I did his.

"Hey Paul what's good?" I said facing my laptop screen.
"Everything's cool. What about on your end?" he asked.
"Just the usual. So wassup? You ready to work?"
"Yeah. I got a new opportunity that I think you could be a part of. I want to meet with you and talk. Is that cool?"
"Yeah that's cool. Give me a time and a place."
"You like seafood?" Paul asked.
"Yup. It happens to be my favorite," I replied.
"OK, well lets go to that new spot in D.C."
"Nemo?"
"Yea that spot. You need me to come scoop you?" he smiled.
I shut him down, "no I can meet you there."
"Ard cool. Well what about tomorrow night at eight? Is that good for you?"
"Yup. I'll see you then," I said.
"Bet. You looking good by the way," Paul smiled again.
"Thanks," I said before disconnecting the Skype.

Was it just me, or was he being fresh? Yea he was definitely being flirtatious. But, he also had an awesome business mind. Anything that he had going on, I wanted in. It was sure to be profitable and if I didn't love anything else... I loved a good profit.

I finished up my day at the office then got to the rest of my Friday business. I stopped at the daycare to pick up

payments and drop off checks. I left Summer's overnight bag there so that when Deon picked up Baby Deon, he could take Summer with him too. Once I got home, I forwarded all the weekly finance reports from my NFC (Nannies for Celebrities, my nanny placement business) over to my accountant. I had my driver pick Miracle and Lil Franko up from school. They came in and barely said hello before they asked for money to go to the mall with their friends. Spoiled brats is what they are... Anyway, I was too tired to tell them no because they went shopping the week before, so I just sent them upstairs to grab a couple stacks out of my closet and then I sent them on their merry way.
"Ma can we catch the bus?" Miracle had the nerve to ask.
"Girl it ain't no damn bus stops around here!"
"Can the driver take us in the city to the bus stop?"
"No! And Timmy is gonna go with yall."
"Ma! Nobody ain't gonna bother us! Why we gotta be at the mall with security?
"Because I'm sending yall out the house with three thousand dollars cash. And yall step father is Deon Matteo, the highest paid quarter back for the Baltimore Ravens. Why wouldn't I? Now if you don't want to give me my money back and yall can stay home," I said pouring myself a glass of sweet red wine.

So they huffed, and puffed, and took their narrow asses out the front door just like I thought. I sent Timmy a text telling him to meet my babies at the mall, then I went upstairs and filled up my jacuzzi. Yes! Some peace and quiet! Some time to get tipsy all by my lonesome without Summer sitting in the bathroom being a creep. I got in and sank down into the water. I didn't even care that the back of my hair was getting wet. Just as I started to get all warm and fuzzy all over my phone rang. It was Paul.
"You busy?" he asked
"No just relaxing in my jacuzzi. Do we need to reschedule dinner?"
"Oh naw. I just wanted to hear your voice that's all," he said.
"Oh really? What did I tell you before Paul. Business and

pleasure... It doesn't mix. We have to keep that separate," I said taking another sip from my glass.

"I figured that was your way of brushing me off since you were married."

"No Paul. That was another reason *along* with the fact that I'm married."

"But you're separated right?" Paul quizzed.

"Who told you that?"

"People talk," he replied.

"Well... Yes, I am," I confessed.

"So how about you let me come over there and make you some breakfast tomorrow morning," Paul suggested.

"What? Breakfast? Nobody touches my stove in my house but me," I responded.

"Well I'm not going to ask to come over there right now... I don't want you to think I'm trying to make a move on you-"

"But you are though. Ray Charles could see that."

"Rose... Just let me come cook you breakfast. We can chat for a little bit... Then I'll leave. I won't wear out my welcome. Then we can still go out to dinner later on."

  A part of me wanted to say no, but it would be nice to have some company though. Lil Franko and Miracle would be at boxing and dance practice in the morning so I would have the house to myself for a little while anyway... So why not?

"I don't know Paul."

"What's not to know? Just give me a chance Rose. I'm not trying to rush you into anything. I won't try anything," Paul promised.

"OK. Ten 'o'clock. I'll send you my address in the morning," I finally agreed.

  I knew two things for sure after our conversation was over. One: Paul was trying to get a sniff of this Rose. Two: Either Deon or LeVelle was telling everybody and their mother that we were separated. I really didn't think that was anybody's business. But it was no sense in me getting upset about it because it was already out and there was nothing I could do about it. Plus, it wasn't like it was a lie. So whatever.

I had a severe case of butterflies. I was going to have a man in my house that wasn't Deon... And he was going to be cooking in y kitchen. I must've been lonely. Seriously. Before I could sit my phone back down on the bathroom floor a text came through form Deon. I was a picture of him with Summer and Baby Deon. Under the picture he texted, "I miss you."

I chuckled a little. Yeah I bet. I thought about the week that I had and a huge grin spread across my face.
"I guess I still got it," I said aloud to myself.

CHAPTER 12
Paul

The next morning I woke up and got my kids ready for practice. I sent them out of the house with homemade bacon, egg, and cheese sandwiches, and orange juice in their water bottles. I watched my driver pull out of the driveway and then I hurried upstairs to get myself ready for Paul to arrive. I wanted to look nice, but not like I was trying to hard. I didn't want to look pressed because I wasn't. I wanted some company, but didn't want to be in my kitchen in a teddy and some high heels. So, I got in the shower and washed my weave then towel dried it, and left it curly. I stood in front of my closet trying to figure out what to wear. I hated having on clothes when I was in the house. It just didn't feel natural to me. But I couldn't have my silk robe on with him over there either so I had to put on something. Why did I tell him he could come over again? My phone vibrated on the night stand and I went to check it. I glanced at the time it was ten o'clock. And just like clockwork, it was a text from Paul. I opened it.

Paul
4438026072
I'm at the gate.

Well at least he was punctual. But that wasn't any help to me in that situation, because I still wasn't dressed. I punched in the security code to open the front gate, then hurried back to my closet. I grabbed a loose fitting gray crop top, and a pair of low rise skinny jeans. I didn't bother putting on any shoes, I hate shoes anyway. I mean I like them with a nice outfit, but when I'm home I'd much rather be bare foot. Anyway, I skipped down the stairs and got to the front door way.

"Hey beautiful," he said as I opened the door.

He handed me a bouquet of red roses. I guess red roses were a universal gift for me since my name was Rose. I didn't let him know that I wasn't impressed though.

"Thank you that was nice of you," I replied. "Come on in."

I looked down and saw bags at his feet.

"Oh. You have groceries? I didn't know you were bringing

anything I have plenty of stuff to cook."

"How can I ask you to come over and cook you breakfast and then cook *your* food? That's ghetto," he chuckled.

Paul picked up the bags and followed me inside.

"This is a very nice house," he complimented.

"Thank you."

I walked him to the kitchen and he sat down his grocery bags on the counter. He walked over to the kitchen sink and washed his hands. I cringed a little on the inside when he dried his hands on the decorative kitchen towels. I didn't allow that... That's what the paper towels were for. But he didn't know, so I decided to give him a pass.

"I was about to ask you where you kept your pots and pans, but I see them right here," he said.

I sat down at the table. I wanted to see this with my own eyes. Deon couldn't cook, so watching a man cook me a whole breakfast was going to be interesting. He started to unload the bags. There was a carton of eggs, milk, orange juice, cinnamon sugar, vanilla extract, grits, butter, cheese, syrup, white bread, and turkey bacon. I giggled in my head. I couldn't remember the last time I had laid eyes on a loaf of white bread. But again, I wasn't going to rain on his parade. I was just going to sit back and watch him do his thing. From the looks of things he was planning on making french toast, cheese eggs, turkey bacon, and grits. I kicked myself in the butt silently because I knew this was against my new no carb diet that I had been falling off all week. I just couldn't get right.

"The bowls are in the cabinet right over top of your head. The spatulas and stuff are in the drawer right in front of you," I said.

So Paul started cooking. And he wasn't too bad, besides the fact that it took a while to get done... And he was a bit messy. I sat on my OCD and kept the mood light though. We chatted about Violet walking in his fashion show that he had coming up. I liked the idea. This would be her first time being in one of his shows. She had always been in his ad campaigns, but never a show.

Finally the food was done and I was ready to eat. Everything looked OK for the most part. The eggs were a little well, I'll say it... Unattractive... Nope, I pride myself in being honest so... THE EGGS WERE UGLY AS HELL. That was one of my biggest pet peeves when it came to breakfast. Some ugly ass eggs! They looked like pebbles on my plate. YIKES. But I appreciated the effort.

"So how's the food?" he asked as we ate.

"Pretty good," I said. "But the next time I would prefer pork bacon," I remarked.

"Oh yea? You eat pork?"

"Yes indeed. I sure do. Pork bacon, pork sausage, pork chops, pork loin, pork roast, ham... All of it!" I laughed. "Let me guess, you don't?"

"Nope," Paul replied.

"Why? You a Muslim?"

"Naw. I just read a lot and I saw how unhealthy it is for you. Don't get me wrong, when I smell some body frying up some pork bacon or some chops I be wanting it so bad, because I remember how good it tastes... But if I even try to eat it I get a headache. My body ain't even used to it no more," he said.

"Dag," I replied.

"I know."

So we finished up breakfast and I washed the dishes. I packed up the left over groceries for Paul to take with him but he declined.

"There you go with the ghetto stuff," he said. "I'm not about to take home stuff that I brought here to cook."

So I put the stuff up in the refrigerator, and when he wasn't looking I threw the loaf of bread in the trash. My house was a potato bread house. Hahaha. Paul left around a quarter after one, which was right on time because Franko and Miracle got home at one thirty. After I made them some homemade chicken alfredo for lunch, I went up to my bedroom for a good ole nap.

I woke up to Lil' Franko asking me if he could hold my card so he pre-order some new video game that was coming out. Yes, my kids knew how to order things off line with a credit card. They were really growing up on me. When they were home they hardly ever bothered me, unless they wanted me to cook, or if they wanted money. Ha! Miracle was on her phone all day, or she was in her room blasting her music. And of course my boy was playing video games or watching sports on ESPN. So anyway, I handed him my card then looked at my phone. It was already six thirty! I had to find something to wear, beat my face, do something to my hair, and drive to D.C. by eight!

 My name could've been Clark Kent that night... I showered, got dressed, and got in the car in the blink of an eye it seemed like. I had a heavy foot any way, so when I was in a rush to get somewhere I pretended that I was a driver for NASCAR. I pulled up to Nemo, and parked at the valet slot. I took a few minutes just to look at my face one more time in my rear view mirror. I had only had enough time to throw some tinted moisturizer on my face and some deep plum lipstick on my lips. Oh, and and some mascara. I had wet my hair a little and put some mousse in it to define the curls a bit. Getting curly hair this time around had been a God send, because when I didn't have time to flat iron I could wear it curly and I would still look cute. I looked away from my mirror and realized that the valet had been holding my door open for me. How long had he been standing there anyway? I didn't have a clue. I stuffed my driver's license in my bra and got out of the car. The valet handed me my ticket, and I stuffed that in my bra as well. Don't judge me, my bra served as my wallet and/or purse when I don't feel like carrying one. Anyway, I walked toward the restaurant's entrance tugging on the bottom of my olive green body con dress so that it wouldn't rise up too much as I walked. It was already eight fifteen, so I figured Paul was already there. I walked up to the hostess, who wore black pants, a black shirt, and a black bow tie.

"Hi," I said.

"Hello, what name is your reservation under?"

"Paul Mackey," I replied.

"OK. Follow me," she directed.

We walked through the main dining room, which was gorgeous. There were enormous fish tanks built into the walls, with baby sharks swimming around in them. The whole place was illuminated by candle light. It was a really nice restaurant. I trailed behind her as we cleared a doorway and up a staircase of about ten steps. Finally, we were on what looked like the rooftop. I looked over to my immediate right, and there was Paul, grinning from ear to ear.

"You look beautiful," he said as he pulled out my chair.

"Thank you," I smiled.

"Those are some bad ass shoes," Paul said looking down at my feet. "What are they?"

"Giuseppe," I said glancing down at my gold strappy heels.

"You have good taste. I like that," Paul complimented.

"Thanks. This is really nice," I responded.

"I thought you would like being up here. It's kind of private. You see it's only like two other tables up here."

I looked around and just as he said there were two other tables. One to the far left, and one in the center, which were both occupied. The backdrop was so pretty. It was like we were sitting right underneath the stars, and the weather was perfect. It was the end of May, and the air was warm and not the least bit damp.

"So... you're late," he chuckled.

"Yeah, I know... I took a nap. I was really tired."

"You were stuffed from that good breakfast," Paul bragged.

I smiled, but didn't even bother to comment. The food wasn't all that. It was good for a man to have cooked. But he was no chef. It was nothing to write home about. Bragging about things that weren't worth bragging about. Not good.

I was glad that the conversation shifted, because I didn't want to have to put his rocky eggs on blast. We discussed the possibility of me partnering up with him for his newest business venture, which was a mentoring program for teenagers. This was definitely an area of interest for me, because I had a lot of advice and words of wisdom to give. And

I loved the idea of showing others that it's not about how you start, but it's all in how you finish. After a few glasses of wine, the business dinner floated into the personal zone.

"What is a total turn off for you in a man?" he asked.

"Lying," I said without a single thought. "I hate liars."

"Wow," he said taking a sip from his drink.

"Oh. And someone who isn't supportive. A significant other who is a low key hater. And jealousy. That's a complete turn off. Don't make me feel bad for being successful or being beautiful. That's not a bad thing."

"True. I like my woman to be just a great as I am... And I love when I have a beautiful woman. I'm the type of guy who will smack you on your ass and whisper in your ear in a bar full of other dudes just so they know that's me. Shit makes me feel good," he chuckled.

"You're crazy," I giggled taking a sip from my daiquiri. "You seem like a good man. So why are you single?"

"Because I haven't had anybody to hold my attention," he answered with no hesitation. "The world is run by social media now. You see somebody on Facebook, they look one way. You meet them in person they look totally different. I met this one girl on Facebook. In her pictures she was so pretty. Took her out one day, and the first thing I see is all these damn bumps on her face. I mean it was like connect the dots on her face. It was terrible."

I bust out laughing. Paul was a fool.

"For real," he went on. "But on a more serious note, most women I run into don't have much going for themselves. I want somebody who has just as much drive as I do. I don't want anybody that just wants to sit on their ass, because I don't just sit on my ass. I go out and get it. When I get an idea, I act on it. When I started my clothing line, you know what I did?"

"What?" I asked.

"I went and took a sewing class so I could hand make all the stuff myself. Then when stuff really got poppin', I went ahead and took it a step further and started paying people to work for me. I'm not lazy at all. And it seems like everybody I meet is just lazy. So that's why I'm single.

"Well hey. You shouldn't settle for anything so I feel you... Totally," I said stuffing a piece of calamari in my mouth.

"Well since you haven't asked me what turns me off, I'm going to tell you," Paul said. "I hate a woman that can't wash clothes."

"What?" I asked.

"I don't like when a woman doesn't know how to wash clothes. I have custody of my son. One time I got him back from his mother, she told me she had washed his clothes that he had worn over the weekend... But when I went in the bag the clothes were like stiff and... I don't know... After you wash clothes I should be able to tell.. They shouldn't be all rough… And they should smell good and not be dingy. They should smell fresh! I be like where's the Bounce Beads and the Oxy Clean?"

We both laughed. Paul was fun to be around. He had good conversation and I liked that. So dinner continued on and the mood was light. We bounced around ideas for our business ventures and our convos drifted elsewhere for brief stints. As dinner came to a close, I finished up my cocktail as he took care of the bill. And then came the foolishness.

"So how are you?" the Caucasian woman asked him as she sat down beside me at the table.

Assuming that Paul knew her, I thought nothing of her inviting herself to our table.

"I'm good," he said nervously.

"So what's this?" she asked him.

"What?" he responded with a question.

"What's this?" she repeated herself.

"What do you mean? This is business," he replied.

"Oh? Business? On a rooftop with candlelight?"

So she turned to me and extended her hand. I shook it, still trying to piece together what was going on.

"Hi. My name is Rose. I'm Paul's wife," she said.

The fact that she said her name was Rose confused me. Then on top of that she said she was Paul's wife. I was shocked

to say the least. In the past two years that I had worked with Paul, I had never seen a wedding band on his finger. In fact, he didn't have one on at dinner that night either. She broke my blank stare with her next question.
"Did you know he was married?"
"No," I replied honestly.
"Oh you didn't? "she asked staring back at him.
"No. Now that I think about it, there was no reason for me to know. I've had a business relationship with him for about two years now, so his personal relationship status really hasn't had a reason to come up."
"Oh OK," she said before she focused her attention back to him. "So why don't you have on your ring?"
"Rose I haven't worn my ring since we've been separated you know that stop acting like you don't know," Paul said.
"But you to told me you were going to a bachelor party," she said.
"I am after I finish up here," he responded.

The two bickered back and forth and I sat there and watched. At this point the nosy person in me had kicked in and I really wanted to see what happened next. As I sat there getting my dose of some needed tea, I felt a tap on my shoulder. I turned around to see a middle aged black woman, with a clippered hair cut smiling ear to ear.
"Yes," I said to her annoyed that my nosiness was being interrupted.
"Hi. Can I speak to you for a minute?" the woman asked.
"Sure," I said.

We walked out into the restaurant's hallway near the main entrance.
"OK. So wassup?" I asked her.
"I just wanted to ask you to step out here just in case things started to get ugly in there," she said.
"Ugly how? Oh wasn't nothing going to get ugly with her towards me," I said on the defensive.
"No. Not with you. With him. First let me introduce myself. My name is Linda."

"Hi I'm Rose," I said to her.
"Rose?" she asked.
"Yes. I thought the same thing when she introduced herself to me in there," I replied.
"Okayyyyy...." Linda giggled. "Well I'm Rose's friend. We were out couponing when she got a phone call that her husband was here having dinner with another woman... So we had to put down our mouthwash and soap and get on on over to see what was going on."
"Hmmm.. OK." I said nonchalantly.
"So, you never knew he was married?" she pried.
"Nope. I didn't have a clue, I've been doing business with him for about two years. Today was my first time ever hearing or seeing anything about him having a wife" I replied.
"Wow. So he never mentioned her?"
"No."

At this point I was irritated. I didn't have time for this mess. I needed to get over to Violet's so I could speak with her about doing the Victoria Secret fashion show. I had given all three of them enough of my time.
"Well look. I have things to do, so I'm out of here," I told Linda as I headed for the door.
"Oh OK. Thanks for speaking with me. And those are some cute shoes you have on."
"Thanks," I said clearing the door.

She had really asked me to come out into the hallway to see if she could get some scoop from me. Well it didn't happen. Then she tried to patronize me by complimenting my shoes. Yeah right. I walked past Paul and his wife on my way to my car. The two argued as he smoked a cigarette. Yuck. He smoked. Another thing I didn't know. As I reached for the driver's side door, Rose called out to me.
"Hey, can I talk to you for a second?"
"No you can't. I don't want to be in the middle of this stupidity. That's your husband. Talk to your husband."
"I mean I didn't come off at you wrong, I talked to you respectfully," she said.

"That's fine. But there is nothing else for you and I to talk about. Like I just said, that is your husband so talk to your husband."

I got in my car and drove off. That whole scene was just weird. My mind hit the rewind button to all the times Paul used the word ghetto in those past days. But not one time did he even think to mention his ghetto ass wife. That's right, I said it. She was a ghetto hot mess. You don't have to be black to be ghetto, I don't care what nobody says. Look how things had played out... All I could do was thank God. He had shown me everything that I needed to know about Paul that fast. I wondered if I should have told his wife that Paul had been pushing up on me. I decided that I had done the right thing. There was no point in giving those microscopic details. Nothing had happened between us, and the original purpose of our dinner was business, so it was cool.

CHAPTER 13
This Girl * Rolls Eyes *

I pulled into Violet's garage and parked, then entered the building. I took the elevator up the the 8th floor and let myself in the house with my key.
"V?" I called out to her.
"Hey Rosie I'm in the kitchen," Violet answered back.
I walked into the kitchen and there was Violet sitting at the table with a plate full of tomatoes in front of her.
"Hey how was your day?" she asked me.
"Girl… So I went to dinner with Paul."
"You mean the one who you always book me with?" V asked.
"Yup. Him. So we went to dinner to discuss working on a line collaboration."
"Oh yea?"
"Yea. So anyway. He's been trying to get at me, but I've been kind of leery because you know mixing business and pleasure is not the way to go."
"Right."
"So I've been kind of wrestling with giving him a chance. So any who, we were at dinner. We talked business. Every now and again, the conversation drifted off… But for the most part it was business. Well at the end of dinner some white lady comes and sits next to me at our table."
"What?"
"Yes. But check this out. It was his wife."
"WHAT?"
"Yes girl. And guess what her name is?"
"Oh goodness. What?"
"Rose."
Violet burst into laughter. I couldn't help but to laugh too. I was glad that I could have a sense of humor about the situation.
"So look. She started asking me questions, you know the normal did I know he was married that type of thing. I let her know that I didn't and while I was being nosy watching her lean on him, her home girl taps me on the shoulder and asks me

to step out and talk to her," I went on. "So basically all she was trying to do was get some dirt but you know I wasn't going to give her none even if there was some to give."
"Damn Rosie that's crazy," Violet replied.
"I know right. I had just told him that I hated liars… And then that shit happened. Oh well," I said.
"So what she look like? Well besides white," Violet laughed.
"Girl… She wasn't a boss white bitch… She had on some picnic able cloth pattern cargo shorts… And she had some wet looking blond hair with grown out roots… Her hair came to her ears… Looks like she gets curly perms… Thin ass eyebrows… Shaped like an egg… Nothing special."
"Oh my God! So I guess his shot has dwindled to nothing huh?" Violet laughed some more.
"And you know it," I chuckled. "So look I really came over here to talk business with you. They want you for the Victoria Secret show."
"Oh really?" Violet asked shaking salt on onto one of the tomato slices.
"Well I thought you would be excited about it."
"I love tomatoes and salt," V said stuffing a heavily salted tomato in her mouth.

  Something wasn't right. I stared at her, trying to put my finger on what was different about her. Her chest looked a little plumper… Her cheeks were a little puffy… I squinted my eyes and the light bulb went off.
"What?" Violet asked salting the next tomato wedge.
"Are you pregnant?" I asked her.
"No," Violet said looking down at her plate.
"Violet don't lie to me," I said.
  Violet chewed up another tomato and swallowed still looking down at her plate.
"So how far along are you?" I asked her.
"I don't know if I'm pregnant," Violet finally responded.
"Well did you have your cycle?" I asked.
"It's late."
"How late?"

"Thirteen days."
"Thirteen days? Girl you are pregnant!"
"You don't know that!" Violet screamed back.
"Are you being for real Violet? Your titties are swollen. Your face is fat. And you are sitting at this table eating tomatoes and salt like it's the best thing on earth! I have been pregnant four times! I know what a pregnant woman looks like, even in the earlier stages! So don't try to play me!" I yelled.
"Well so what! I'm grown! So what if I'm pregnant! I have money I can take care of my baby!"
"V. Did you forget that you are a super model? Do you realize that you will not be able to walk down nobody's runway in stilettos when your feet and ankles are so swollen that you can't even put a shoe on?"
"I'll worry about that when the time comes," Violet replied nonchalantly.
"V. Baby. You have your whole life to have a baby. Right now you have a career that is taking you so many places. Why would you want to jeopardize that?"
"Why do you make it sound like having a baby is such a bad thing? You have kids!"
"This is not about me in case you don't understand who we're talking about here. We're not talking about me. I am not a model. I sit behind the desk. I collect the money. I don't have to be in front of a camera. Therefore, if I blow up it doesn't matter."
"Look. It's my life and my career. If I want to have a baby then that's my business," V responded.
  This girl must've lost her damn mind. For the life of me I just couldn't understand why she would want to put her whole career on hold just to have a baby!
"So who's the father? I asked.
"None of your business," Violet said.
"None of my business?"
"No. It's none of your business," Violet repeated.
"Oh so I guess Young Bread is the father. Right?"
  Violet fell silent. When Violet got silent in a

conversation it meant that she didn't want to tell the truth, but she didn't want to tell a lie either.

"Girl what in the hell is wrong with you? First of all why did you sleep with that boy unprotected? You do know that you are not the only person he's having sex with right? And lets think beyond that. What does this boy have to offer a child?"

"He has kids already. He takes care of his kids," Violet replied.

"OK well fine. How many children does he have?"

"Why does that matter?"

"Just answer the question and I will tell you why it matters," I said.

"Nine."

"Nine kids? Hmmm.. OK. And are they by the same mother?"

"No."

"Oh OK. Now we're getting somewhere. So he has nine kids by I don't know how many different mothers. And now you are pregnant by him. But for whatever reason you think that he is going to be faithful and be a happy family with you and your child even though he hasn't done that on nine other occasions? Now that makes a whole lot of sense," I sarcastically spewed.

"Get out of my house," Violet said.

"Oh so now you're putting me out because I'm doing what I'm known to do... Be real? OK. That's cool. I guess your hormones are getting the best of you. Bye," I said before I got up from the table and left the house.

    And there was another life lesson. Penis has the potential to turn you against your own family. It was really sad. As I drove home I tried to think of a positive outcome concerning the situation. I couldn't think of any. I had a feeling in my gut that this was going to turn out bad. My phone rang and I was kind of glad, this had the potential to interrupt my disturbing thoughts about Violet's pregnancy. Then I looked at the screen. It was Paul. What could he possibly have to talk about after that fiasco at Nemo?

"Hello?"

"Hey," he said.

"Hey? Let me get this off my chest. I asked you why were you single and you answered without even blinking. Not even twenty five minutes later your wife comes and has a seat at our table! That's crazy! I told you how I feel about liars!"

"I know. I know. But I wasn't lying. I am single. Well technically I'm separated from her. We've been separated for like two years now," Paul explained.

"So why couldn't you tell me that? Why did I have to find that out instead of you just telling me?" I asked.

"I don't know. I didn't think it was necessary."

"Really? But here it is, you're talking about pursuing something with me, and you didn't think it was necessary to let me know that you are still legally married? To a woman who obviously feels like there is still something there because she made it her business to pop up on you?"

"I know. I told her I didn't like that."

"When? After I left? And if yall ain't together then why were you explaining yourself to her? And you made sure to tell her it was a business meeting? And don't get it twisted. I'm not about to sit here and get wrapped up in your little games. The only reason I didn't tell her about you coming over and making me breakfast or even about he other parts of our conversations was because it seems like yall got some stuff yall need to work out, and I don't want to be the reason that yall don't. Now I'll tell you this, I'm not going to turn down any opportunities to get a check. But as far as you and I on a personal level, that's dead."

"Rose... I know it seems bad but it's not what you think. We are separated. Why do you think you've never seen me with a ring on? Me and her don't have no ties except the rental properties we have together. We don't have no kids together. None of that."

"The rental properties are enough. That means a divorce is gonna take a while. I ain't got time. Like I said, business wise I'm still on board. But other than that, naw. I'll pass. But you have a nice night and enjoy the bachelor party," I said before I hung up.

CHAPTER 14
The Cat Is Out The Bag

Once a week I flew to Virginia so that I could go with Aunt Lucinda for her radiation treatments. She seemed to be handling the process pretty well. Even if she was feeling the complete opposite, she wouldn't have told me anyway. I had been trying to hold in the fact that Juan had told me everything about the little love triangle they had going on once upon a time, but it was starting to put a strain on me. I wondered if it still bothered Aunt Lucinda. I wondered if when I spoke about my father, in the back of her mind did she wonder if he told me or not.

We sat at the table in the cafe, about to have lunch. Aunt Lucinda said she wasn't hungry, but I really wanted her to eat. She was losing weight, probably from the stress of the whole cancer thing. Her chicken noodle soup came out and she took a sip from her spoon here and there. Juan's facing kept popping up in my mind. It was time for me to free my aunt of that mental burden, because I knew there had to be one. If not, she wouldn't have lied about knowing who my father was in the first place.

"So, how's Violet doing? She don't even call me," my aunt said breaking my thoughts.

"She's good. We get to find out what she's having at her next appointment. I don't know why she won't call you though. I told her you ain't mad, I'm the one that's mad. And I'm not even mad no more to be honest."

"Well I'm glad you're easing up about it," she responded sipping from her cup of tea.

I sprinkled some salt on my salad and again there was Juan's face in my head. I had to get this off my chest. It was time.

"So," I started off. "You know I've been spending time with my father now..."

"Yes. You told me. I'm happy that you two can both be adults and make an honest attempt to mend your relationship," Aunt Lucinda said.

"Thanks. But... Well... We had a long talk... And um... He told me about you and him."

Aunt Lucinda looked down into her bowl. She oozed shame. It was awful. I automatically started kicking myself in the butt silently. The last thing I wanted to do was upset her, given all she was going through at the moment.

"Oh really?"

"Yup."

She began to stir her soup. It was a very awkward moment. She started to speak, and I was glad because I didn't know what else to say. My tongue was truly tied.

"Well, I can't say that I'm proud of that... That was one of the darkest moments in my life. I almost want to say that I regret it, but I don't."

I forced a forkful of caesar salad into my mouth. She had to be kidding me. How could she say that she didn't regret sleeping with her sister's man? Wow. She had big balls today. Real big gigantic heavy ones.

"It drove me right into God's arms," she went on. "Viola wanted nothing else to do with me... So I moved here. All I wanted was her forgiveness. She wasn't trying to hear it though. I'll never forget what she said to me... She said God forgives, but I don't...Humph... So I went to the little church around the corner from my house the next morning... It was a Sunday. I gave my life to Christ and I've never been the same."

And somehow she always found a way to make me feel guilty about being mad at her. Go figure. There was no way I could be upset with her now, not after that touching testimony. Ha!

"Well, we all have secrets Aunt Lucy that's life. Just wanted to let you know that I know so you won't have to continue to carry it that's all. I'm not judging you at all. It's over and done with it's time to move on now," I said taking a sip of my cranberry juice.

After all of that, my day still wasn't over. After I caught my flight back to Baltimore, I had to go to dinner with Violet. Since she was dead serious about having this baby, I had to make sure that she was still going to get work. So it was time to transition her over to maternity modeling. She wasn't too hot on the idea at first, but I had to remind her that if she wanted to sit around and bake a baby for forty weeks, the bills weren't going to stop coming. Plus both she and I knew that dumb ass baby daddy of hers wasn't going to take care of her, so she was going to have to make it happen. I was going to teach her how to be la jefa if it was the last thing that I did. That's what it's all about. Teaching your loved ones how to keep the legacy going.

Anyway, I got to V's condo around five thirty. Lil Franko and Miracle were at home, and Summer was with Deon's mother, so I didn't have any kids to tend to. V came outside looking four months pregnant. There was no way she could hide it. Maternity modeling was definitely what she was going to have to do. My plan was to start shopping her around now, because I didn't want to wait until she was too huge to do anything. That way we could have a few gigs for her by the time she was five no more than five and a half months. That would give her about three months to do her thing, or at least until her doctor said she needed to chill out.

She got in the car and I immediately knew that something was wrong. She had a scowl on her face and her eyes were glued to her phone. I was hoping that it was just a preggo mood swing that she would get over.
"Hey Mommy," I greeted her.

She didn't respond. This was bad. Ever since I had decided to accept the fact that she was pregnant, I would address her as "Mommy". And her face lit up every time I said it. So this couldn't be good.
"What's wrong," I began to probe.

She ignored me again, still looking in her phone.
"Um hello, earth to the pregnant lady in my car... What's the matter with you?" I sang playfully.
"I hate him," she said tearfully.

I figured as much. That was the only thing that could upset her these days. Anything that had anything to do with her fairytale family.

"Oh Lord. What he do?" I cringed.

She handed me her phone. This wasn't going to set us up for a good meeting, I could tell. She was going to be salty for the rest of the day, all because of her chipmunk looking baby daddy.

"Press play," she said.

It only took me a second to realize that I was about to look at an Instagram video. I felt a huge knot in my stomach. Was I going to have to go kill that boy? I pressed the play button. The ugly boy was in the studio. I don't know why because he had no talent. He sucked.

"Super model bitches lined up at my front doe'... Her belly got a pudge but I ain't the Daddy doe'... Think she the shit cuz she pretty and her walk mean'... But I ain't fallin' for it walk it out Billy Jean..." he rapped into the mic.

I looked at the caption which read, "#FreestyleFriday." This boy was a straight up scum bag. Violet sat in the passenger seat, not saying a word. I put Freestyle Friday into the search bar and clicked hash tags. The video had already been reposted like a thousand times. What a lame. What a coward. What a low down, dirty, ugly, talentless, piece of shit he was. Pardon my french.

I wanted to say I told you so to my little sister so bad, but I figured the embarrassment of the situation was enough. She wasted her time with that little bastard for no reason at all. She was putting her career on hold for this poor excuse for a man and he wanted absolutely no parts of this family fantasy that she had dancing around in her head.

"So where do you go from here?" I asked her, really wanting to tell her what to do.

"I don't know," a tear dropped from her eye. "I mean this is just entertainment right?"

I just couldn't understand why Violet couldn't see this scum bag for what he was. He was blatantly disrespecting her. Not just to her face, which wouldn't make it any better... But to the whole world. Nowadays, social media equates to the whole world. Everyone and their great grandmother's uncle's cousin's

daughter had some type of access to social media. Even kids in elementary school have some type of social media account. So for her to still try to make excuses for this man was mind boggling to me. What did he have to do in order for her to purge him from her life? I wish I knew so I could get the ball rolling. I closed my eyes for a second and Franko flashed through my head. Then I was reminded of the life lesson of learning from experience. Sometimes, someone else warning us of what's up ahead just isn't enough. Sometimes, we have to be hard headed and dive head first into five feet anyway. Then once we crack our skulls in that shallow pool, we just might get it. And sometimes unfortunately, we have to take that silly dive a few times before we fully understand. I felt like this situation was one of those times. I took a deep breath.
"I don't know V. Maybe. But I'll tell you what I found out from my own experience. Now you can do what you want with this... A man who truly loves you isn't going to intentionally disrespect you or humiliate you."

V said nothing so I said nothing else. I handed her back her phone and shifted the car back into drive. She burst in to tears, and it broke my heart. I wanted to kill that boy ten times, then kill him again. But for what? Just so she could go dig him out of the grave and give him mouth to mouth? Nope. I couldn't get involved. It would eventually drive a wedge between her and I, and I didn't want that. I had to let her get to her breaking point, just like she had done with Andrew. She had to finally say enough is enough, I couldn't decide that for her.

Just as I suspected, my sister was a stick in the mud for the rest of the evening. I told her all the plans that I had for her, yet all I could get out of her was, "uh huh... Oh okay." When I just couldn't take anymore, I wrapped dinner up and carried her pregnant broken hearted behind on home. I knew she was hurt, but what I wasn't gonna do was sit and dwell on it. She could do that by herself on her own time. Truth is, as a woman when you decide to have a baby in this day and age you have to mentally prepare yourself for the possibility of having to do it on your own. Things just aren't how they used to be.

Nowadays, even marriage can't make a man be a daddy. This generation of men don't have a clue on how to be men. Not all of them, but the vast majority of them. All they want to do is run around with multiple women and then leave them with the seeds that they sprinkled. Not just babies... But the soul ties that they leave behind. The stuff that keeps women up at night tossing and turning while they are across town in another woman's bed. The stuff that will drive a woman crazy. The stuff that will make a woman pick up all sorts of habits that they never had before. That stuff that can make her yearn for him even when she has called herself moving on to someone else. That mental agony.

We as women sometimes don't even think about what we are actually opening ourselves up to when we open up to another man without tapping into our ability to feel out a man's vibes. That God given gift that only we have. WOMEN'S INTUITION. We will get with a man and all types of alarms will go off in our heads. God will send us all types of signs. But we will go on and jump in head first anyway, knowing that something isn't right. Then wonder why things didn't work out once they fall apart. That's just crazy. Just like I saw all that stuff on the internet about her little boyfriend, I know Violet did too. It was no way she didn't, she was a social media junkie. So just like I knew he was a dog, so did she. It wasn't like he did a good job hiding it. Every other day he was with a different chic, so what did Violet expect?

Oh I know what she expected. She expected for him to change because she was different! She just knew that she could make him a better man because her vagina was made of diamonds and pearls... And sadly, my little sister was not the only woman who has done this. All of us have done it, or will do it before our time on this earth expires. What am I speaking of you ask? TRYING TO CHANGE A MAN WHO HAS NO DESIRE TO CHANGE. We would rather break our necks and backs bending over backwards for men who just don't care about anybody but themselves. They aren't there yet, but for some reason we are convinced that we can make them be there. It takes a lot of growth and maturity to accept the fact that no matter how hard you may want to, you can't change anybody but yourself. Bottom line. And until Violet understood that, she was going to be crying forever.

I watched her walk into her building and then I pulled off. The meeting with her didn't make me feel productive at all. I needed a pick me up. I picked up my phone and began to dial.
"Hello Mrs. Matteo, what do I owe you for the privilege of hearing your voice this evening?"
"Good evening Mr. Madrid. Just calling to see if you could still get me in contact with your friend who has the lingerie line. Is that possible?" I asked Mr. Madrid.
"Yes Mam. Let me get on that right now," he replied.

CHAPTER 15
Meeting Nesha

A huge grin spread across my face as I laid my eyes on the contract for my takeover of Voluptueux. Yes you read it right. I met up with Mr. Madrid's business associate, Clyde Warner who was the owner of Voluptueux. Once he saw me in person and heard all the things I had my hands (and money) in... He just had to have me come aboard... And he wanted me to do more than just be a body for his campaign relaunch. He offered me the position of CEO of the company, once I bought it from him of course. Turns out, he was completely tired of running the company. He wanted to focus his attention on his interior design business. According to him he was no longer passionate about lingerie, and he wanted to sell the company to someone who he felt could take it to another level. I didn't even think twice about it once he offered. I mean why not? I had the money, and with the type of drive I had I could accomplish anything. I know that may sound cliché, but it's true. I wanted it all. And I wanted it all to be my own. Not trying to be selfish, but I didn't want anybody to be able to say they fed me. I wanted to eat off my own table. I had to be the boss. My father told me I was La Jefa, so I had to continue to live up to that.

Signing new deals always made me happy. Even though my lawyer always raked over all my paperwork with a fine tooth comb, I still liked to read over everything as well. I slipped on my reading glasses and jumped right on in. The contract wreaked of fresh money and I loved it. My desk phone rang and to my surprise, Rochelle's number popped up in the caller I.D. window. I thought for a second. Should I answer it? "Rose speaking," I said into the receiver after I placed it to my ear.
"Wow. I didn't think you were going to answer," Rochelle said.
"Well yeah, I've been busy," I replied.
"I suppose. And I think you've been avoiding me too. But that's OK. I already know how your pride makes you shut people out and all that jazz. I was just calling to see how you were."
"I'm very well I can't complain," I responded.

"Oh OK... Well that's good to hear," Rochelle said.

The phone grew quiet. I knew Rochelle. I knew that she wanted to know what my current status was with Deon, but she didn't want to seem as if she were prying. But that conversation was a bit personal, and I felt more comfortable speaking about that in person if at all. The whole scenario was still kind of sore to the touch.

"So... What's on your agenda for today?" I quizzed.

"Nothing too heavy... I'm on my way to lunch," Rochelle stated.

"Where?"

"I'm in the mood for seafood, so I'm thinking The Bay Bridge."

"Oh OK. I'm feeling a little famished, do you want me to meet you over there?" I asked.

"Yeah sure if you want to," Rochelle answered.

"OK. I'm on my way."

I forwarded my calls to Lexi's desk (I hate checking my voice mail) and headed out to lunch. I always enjoyed my time out with Rochelle. She always had a funny story to tell. I needed a laugh anyway. Finally, I had my listening ear back. I arrived to The Bay Bridge around one. It was a beautiful day. The valet opened my door and I stepped out of my car feeling fabulous. That was good, because the past couple of days I had been up and down. Mostly down thinking about Deon. I felt somewhat defeated. But now wasn't the time for gloom and doom. If I did decided to spill the beans about my pending divorce, then I was going to keep it light. I didn't want to dampen our lunch session with regrets and bitterness. I would save that for my conversations that I often had with myself.

I walked into the restaurant and I immediately saw Rochelle. She was sitting at a table but she wasn't alone. I had no idea that this was going to be a lunch for three. I walked right past the hostess before she could even get a chance to ask me how many were in my party. I approached the table and Rochelle's face brightened when she saw me.

"Hey!" she said chipperly.

"Hey girl," I said with a smile.
"Well come on sit down over here beside me," she continued on.

I sat down in the chair beside Rochelle and my eyes shifted to the other side of the table. I hadn't seen this woman before. She looked at me with a fake smile, trying to size me up a bit. But she quickly realized that she wasn't on my level... I could tell.

"Hi I'm Nesha," she said extending her hand.

I shook it, still not sure what to think of her. There was something going on there, I just couldn't quite put my finger on it.

"Oh I'm sorry! I'm so rude," Rochelle chirped. "This is my best friend Rose. Rose this is my good girlfriend Nesha."

"It's nice to meet you Nesha," I lied.

I'm sorry yall, but I am very skeptical of meeting new people. I know that sounds crazy, being that I come in contact with new people all the time... But I really try to shield myself from new personal interactions. Business is business, so meeting new people is inevitable. But inviting people into my personal space, I'm not too big on that.

"Likewise," Nesha replied.

She gave Rochelle a crazy look, but I guess she thought she was doing it on the slide. Too bad I was all over it, so she couldn't get anything past me.

"You didn't tell me we were having company," Nesha said to Rochelle.

"Oh I'm sorry, I didn't realize we were at someone's house. I thought this was a restaurant," I butted in.

"Girl you crazy!" Rochelle laughed trying to lighten the mood.

Nesha joined in on the laughter, but I didn't. I didn't see where the joke was in what I said, because I wasn't playing at all. Don't come for me, especially if I didn't send for you.

"We already put our appetizers in," Rochelle said to me.

"Oh OK, well as soon as the waitress comes back I'll be ready to put mine in," I responded.

I picked up my menu and skimmed through the

appetizers. I decided on a cup of cream of crab soup to start off.
"Oh! So *you're* Rose? Shelly told me about your modeling business. I got a lot of connects on that, so if you need my help just let me know," Nesha said.
"Who is Shelly?" I asked.
"Me girl," Rochelle laughed. "That's what they used to call me when I was growing up."
"Oh really?"
"Yup. I've known Shelly for over thirty years. But anyway, like I was saying if you need me to help you get in the door as far as the modeling industry goes just let me know," Nesha said proudly.

Get my foot in the door? Wait a minute. Did this girl just offer me help in something that I was already eating off of... Big time? Rochelle couldn't have told her that much, because if she did then she would know that I was doing my thing already.
"Oh I'm good already."

I started to run down my whole resume, but I didn't. I didn't have a thing to prove to her. Truth be told, if she was that in tune with the modeling world then she would already know the checks I was out there getting. It was no need to bust her in her head with all my accomplishments. Not at this moment anyway. I would always have that in the arsenal just in case though.

The waitress brought out Rochelle and Nesha's cocktails and appetizers. Rochelle ordered seafood potato skins, and Bonita ordered fries. Fries for her appetizer. Right. So anyway, I put in my order and sipped on my water while I waited.
"Rosie, you want one of these?" Rochelle pointed at her potato skins.
"I wish I could... But I'm on this no carb diet. So the potatoes I can't do. I probably shouldn't have got that soup either now that I think about it. They probably used flour to thicken it," I responded.
"Well more power to you. 'Cuz I don't do know diets. I just

walk to keep the shape that God gave me," Nesha said getting up from the table. "I'll be back I have to go o the bathroom."

I watched her walk away to get a glimpse of this glorious shape that only needed walking to keep in tact. Sadly, I didn't see it. Her "shape" kind of reminded me of a capital letter P. Straight down the back, and the hump in the front. Skinny ass legs. But hey, who was I to have an opinion? She was confident, so that's all that mattered right? In the middle of me chuckling to myself about Ms. Not Having No Shape Nesha it hit me. I knew her name sounded familiar!

"Ain't that the chick you told me about that was going between you and your other friend being messy and keeping shit going?" I asked.

"Yeah that's her," Rochelle replied.

"And you're back friends with *her*? You trust her?"

"People make mistakes Rose you say it all the time. Forgiveness. Ain't that what you always preach?"

"Yes it is. I didn't say you couldn't forgive her, but you don't have to allow her back into your personal space either," I said.

"Well that's what I choose to do and I'm cool with it so that's all that matters," Rochelle snapped.

"Okay Rochelle it's no need to get smart I'm just trying to protect you that's all."

"Well I'm good."

At this point I was pissed. Rochelle was defending this girl like she was sleeping with her or something. It was weird. And I didn't like the bean bag shaped heifer either which made it even worse. And at that moment, I just wanted to get out of there. I felt like this lunch date was going left and I ain't have the time for it. I could be at my office reading over the contract for Voluptueux. I didn't need to be a part of this foolishness. I grabbed my clutch and and pulled out a twenty.

"Yeah so I'm just going to go ahead and leave," I said placing the money on the table.

"What?" Rochelle asked.

I got up from the table and without saying anything else, I exited the restaurant. There was no need for me to be there. I drove down the street and grabbed myself a salad and carrot juice, then headed back to work. On my way there, of course Rochelle called. But I wasn't interested in hearing her voice. She could enjoy her lunch with her snakeish funny built friend. I was over it. I had went this long without speaking to her, so I could survive without her friendship.

CHAPTER 16
Self Evaluation

After my work day was over, I rounded up the kids from daycare and after school activities and went on home. When I pulled up to the security gate, Rochelle's car was sitting there. What did she want? I didn't have anything to say to her. Oh, but I was going to fix her. I was going to ignore her so hard that she was going to start questioning her own existence. I reached my hand out of my window and punched in the code to the gate. It opened and I drove in. Rochelle trailed behind me in her car. I parked the car in the garage and reminded the kids of what needed to be done once we got in the house. Homework, the gathering of their uniforms for the next day... You know those type of thing. I always told them what they needed to to before we got in the house. That way they could get straight to it without me having to get their attention once they got in the house.

"Mommy Aunt Rochelle is here," Summer said in her cute little voice.

"I know baby" I said as I got out of the car.

I lifted her from her car seat, positioned her on my hip, and shut the car doors. Miracle and Lil' Franko got out of the car and waved to Rochelle. She waved back as she go out of her car.

"Can I talk to you for a second?" Rochelle called out to me.

I walked toward the door without making any type of eye contact with Rochelle. This pissed her off, I could tell.

"So you're gonna act like you don't hear me?"

I walked in the house and shut the door without blinking. I sat Summer down at the table and went to the cabinet to find her a snack. The doorbell rang as I reached for a pack of fruit snacks. She really didn't know how to just go on about her business when somebody was ignoring her, now did she? I walked over to the window and there Rochelle was standing on the front doorstep with her arms crossed. She turned around and saw me standing at the window. I rolled my eyes, then closed the curtains. There was nothing to talk to her about.

"I'm not leaving until you come out here and talk to me!" I heard her scream.

"Summer go upstairs with Miracle," I told Summer.

"OK."

She jumped down from her chair and did what she she was told fruit snacks and juice box in hand. I went out front. This girl had lost her damn mind.

"What?" I asked full of irritation.

"Why is it so easy for you to stop being my friend?" Rochelle asked.

"What?"

"You heard me. Every time something happens, the first thing you do is cut me off. Even when I didn't do anything wrong. Then you just come back like ain't nothing happen. That ain't right," Rochelle stated.

"Stop talking out the side of your neck," I replied.

"What? You got amnesia? You need examples?"

"Cut the dramatics," I said as I turned my back on her and walked toward my front door.

"OK since you act like you're oblivious to what I'm saying. You cut me off several times when you were getting high, when all I was trying to do was help you. Then it happened again when Deon cheated with Michelle. Next it was when the stuff happened between me and his brother in Hawaii for Summer's birthday. Then you disappeared off the face of the earth when Deon called my phone. And now you're doing it all over again and we haven't even been back speaking for not even five hours! I'm starting to wonder if you are *really* my friend! Because you throw me away at the drop of a dime!" Rochelle screamed.

Her words stopped me in my tracks. As dramatic as her whole speech had been, I had to recognize truth when there was truth. And maybe it was a little wrong of me for treating Rochelle that way. She had been my only friend when I moved back to Baltimore from Virginia. She had been there for me through everything I had been through. She had been there for me through everything. Me terminating a pregnancy, when I got raped by the guys when I was on the streets, she had even tried to shield me from the darker parts of dancing. She forgave me even after I had stolen from her when I was still struggling with my substance abuse issues. And on top of that, Rochelle didn't have any body close to her. Her son and daughter lived in Atlanta... All of her brothers had been killed... Her mother was in prison and her father had been killed as well. All her life she had been dealing with people leaving her. And here I was with my selfish bratty ways. It was always about me. And that was the truth. It stung a little bit, but it was still the truth. Even though I knew she was right, that spirit in me that always wanted to be right was still lurking... So I had to at least try to attempt to prove her wrong some type of way.

"But some of those times you *were* wrong," was what I came up with.

That was so stupid of me to say. Damn Rose. It sounded much more affective when I said it in my head. I already knew what Rochelle's initial response was going to be.

"So!" came out of her mouth just as I thought she would say it.

Yea it was time for me to put on my girl panties and own up to what I had been doing to someone that I considered to be best friends with. I took a deep breath.

"Come on inside," I said walking into the front door, leaving it open for her.

I went to the kitchen and opened the refrigerator. I took out a jar of olives. They were Rochelle's favorite. I opened the jar, drained the juice then poured some out into a little glass bowl, then slid it across the counter to her along with a fork.

"Thanks," she said.

"You're welcome," I said.

Rochelle ate her olives in silence and I poured us both a glass of moscato. I sat down across from her at the counter. I had something I needed to get something off my chest.

"You're right. As much as I would like for you to be wrong. You're right," I said.

"I'm not your enemy Rosie. I'm your friend. I'M NOT YOUR

ENEMY! You are my family. I don't have anyone else here... Well Nesha... But I just started back talking to her like a week ago. Maybe a little longer. Whatever. That don't even matter. I just don't like feeling like at any given moment you can just drop our friendship like it don't mean shit to you," Rochelle replied.

"I apologize."

Rochelle took a sip from her glass. The she got up from and went back to the refrigerator and grabbed the jar of olives. She replenished her glass bowl, returned the jar to the refrigerator, then sat back down.

"Apology accepted," she said popping another olive into her mouth.

Self examination. Every now and again we all need some. Most of the time we don't want to do it, because deep down we know some of our ways aren't the nicest. But truth be told, we all have some things about ourselves that we need to check. Yes, every now and again we have to check ourselves. And sometimes it will take someone else to bring our bull crap to the light in order for us to address it. It's all a part of being an adult. As a child denial is a part of your daily life. You are young, you are immature, and in your mind it's all about you. But as you become an adult you begin to learn that the world doesn't revolve around you, and you too can be wrong sometimes. And that's not the worst thing in the world. The worst thing is when you realize you are wrong and you do nothing to correct it.

Now lets move on to women and friendships. We can drop friends as soon as they do the slightest things to annoy us. But when we have a man who cheats, lies, is lazy, etc... We feel the need to see it through. Why? We should value friendships the same way as we do relationships. True friends turn into family, and you should always value your family. Always. If you are blessed with a friend who is always there... One that will give you their last and you would do the same for them... One that is always there cheering you on when you reach new heights in life... Who will listen to your same stories about the same dog of a man... And then will give you honest advice on what to do... Who is down to jump in that car and act crazy with you... And will call you out on your mess when you're getting too crazy... You have to hold on to that. There are too many people out here disguising themselves as real friends, when they are only around to see what they can gain from being in your circle. Or they really can't stand you and they are secretly praying for your down fall simply because of jealousy... I say all this to say when you have a true friend and a solid friendship, take it seriously. Don't treat them like they are disposable.

So for the rest of the evening I sat in the kitchen with my best friend catching her up on what had been going on in my life, and she did the same.

CHAPTER 17
A Change of Heart

"I'm separated," he said plain as day.
"Oh Lord another so called separated one," my mind screamed within itself.

Why couldn't the men who pursued me be completely unattached? I didn't want anyone else's man.
"Oh really? Well so am I. But are you really separated or are you just taking a break? You know there is a difference," I said finally.

Yes. I had given in. After having him pop up to my office with Edible Arrangements, sent me emails, call my office phone and even send ten pair of Loubs individually gift wrapped, finally I gave him my cell number. I just hoped that I hadn't made a mistake by doing that.
"No. I'm legally separated. I filed the paperwork. I have my own apartment and everything. If it weren't for the fact that in the State of Maryland you have to be separated for a year, then I would be divorced already."
"Um hum," I hummed into the phone.

With as much crap as I had been through with Deon, and the ghetto confrontation at Nemo with Paul and his wife, I couldn't believe a word that any man said. They said one thing, and then did the other. So I couldn't be sure. Either way, I was just having fun. So if he went back to his wife that day or the next, it wouldn't really matter. I wasn't banking on anything serious between him and I. Plus I couldn't get past the fact that he was one of Deon's team mates. He wasn't getting past my jeans anyway. So the conversation continued on, and he kept me entertained with his wild fan stories. My line beeped three times, all from Deon. I didn't want to hear his voice, so I decided not to answer. He didn't have anything important to say anyway.

After another hour on the phone with Brent, I decided to end the conversation. I didn't want him to get the idea that I was pressed for rap. I had to end the conversation before he did.

"Well, let me get off this phone. I have some things I need to take care of," I lied.
"Oh, OK. I wish you could talk a little longer. I enjoy your conversation," Brent said.
"Oh well, I'll call you in a couple days when I have some free time," I remarked.
"Cool. Yea you are a busy woman."
"Yup. So I'll talk to you soon."
"OK. Bye."

I hung up without returning the bye. Had to leave him cliff hanging. Hahaha. But anyway, I needed to check my voice mails. I hit the recording icon on the top of my phone, and played the first message.
"Rosie please pray for my boy," the voice mail played.

It was Deon. By the sound of terror in his voice I knew there was something serious going on. I called his phone back three times and still no answer. Then I called his mother. If anybody knew what was going on, then she would.
"Hey. Deon left me a crazy message. What's going on?"
"Deonte' almost drowned. I'm here at the hospital now."
"What? Which one?"
"Mt. St. Joseph."
"OK. I'm on my way."

I grabbed my wallet and sprinted to the car. Lord have mercy. How could this have happened? Deonte knew how to swim! All the kids did! I had paid for all of them to have swimming lessons! It was too much for my mind to grasp at that moment. I shifted gears and did the only thing I knew that could help in this type of situation. I prayed.
"Lord I don't know the extent of this situation, but whatever it is I know that you are in control. What I'm asking of you now is for you to wrap your arms around Deonte. No... I know you are already touching him Lord, just hold him a little tighter Lord. I know I don't have the answers and I know that this has happened according to your will... But Lord please let Deonte be OK. In Jesus name I pray... Amen."

Once I got to the hospital, I parked in the garage and

made my way inside. After stopping at the reception desk and obtaining a visitor's badge, I was directed to the floor where Deonte' was. As soon as I stepped off the elevator, I was overcome with sadness. Trina sat in her chair rocking back and forth, eyes blood shot red. Deon was pacing back and forth in the hallway. His mother held his hand as he paced. The rest of Trina's family was in the waiting room as well.
"I got here as soon as I could," I said to Deon as I hugged him.
"Thanks. I appreciate it," Deon said. He looked at his mother, "Ma, you can go ahead and sit down."

As she took a seat, Deon turned and looked at me. I had never seen him this sad in the entire time that I had known him. It broke my heart to see him this way. It was no way I could go through with the divorce. I had to stick by my husband.
"Deon baby what happened?" I asked holding his hands in mine.
"He was at Trina's sister house in the yard. Him and his cousin were playing and chasing each other.. You know how boys play. It was wet out there because they were in and out of the pool I guess. So R.J. Was chasing him and Deonte slipped and fell in the pool-"
"OK but he knows how to swim though," I interrupted.
"Yea he does. But somehow he hit his head on the edge of the pool before he went in," Deon explained.
"Oh my God," I said.
"This shit is hard Rosie if my son don't make it I don't know what I'm going to do," Deon's voice cracked.
"OK. Calm down. Just calm down. What are the doctors saying?"
"Well, nobody can see him right now. They say he's stable for the moment. But it's not looking too good. His brain went a few minutes without oxygen while he was under that water. They say they will have a neurologist look at him in the morning. Now we just have to see if he makes it through the night. It's kind of touch and go."

Wow. You see how quick life can change? I didn't even know what to say! What are the right words to say to someone who is facing the possibility of losing their child? Then I was dealing with my own emotions. Man Man was like one of my own! So I told him the only thing that I knew for sure.

"Deon baby you have to trust God. He will work this whole thing out. But you have to trust him. Do you trust him?"

"Yes, I trust him," Deon said with tears streaming down his face.

I let go of his hands and wiped his tears.

"Come on, let's pray," I said to him.

I grabbed his hands again and closed my eyes. I knew there wasn't anybody who could fix this but God.

"Father God we come as humble and sincere as we know how to come God. We just want to say thank you God. We want to thank you that we are even at this point God. We know if it weren't for your will God that Deonte' could be gone right now God. So for that Father we just want to give you glory God. But right now Lord we just ask that you take it one step further God. We ask that you bring him out. We ask that you heal his body God. I ask that you wrap your arms around his parents Lord. Comfort them God. Remind them that you are God all by yourself and that you have it all under control God. Remind them that you are good and you are merciful Lord God. Keep them strong Lord God. Just let your will be done Lord, because we know you don't make any mistakes. In Jesus name we pray, Amen."

I gave Deon a hug and a kiss. I sat with him for a few hours, then I had to get home. The kids had school and daycare in the morning, and I had to make sure everybody got there. I let Deon know that I would be back the next day. Once I got home and told the kids what was going on, they were devastated. They didn't see Man Man as their stepbrother, they saw him as their blood brother. Everybody had been hurt by this tragic event, which made the blow even harder. Seeing how hard everybody was taking it, really made me pray even harder that we wouldn't lose him. I knew things would go completely left if that were to happen. Nobody would be able to handle that.

All night I tossed and turned. I wished that I could've stayed at the hospital with him... He was really going through it. So when the alarm clock went off at 6:30 a.m. I popped up ready to get the day started. I started breakfast, then got Miracle and Franko up. I always woke Summer up last, because for her to be so little, she wasn't a morning person at all. After everyone had eaten breakfast, they got dressed and we were out the door. I dropped Franko and Miracle off to school, then I took Summer to daycare. By the time this was finished, it was a little after eight thirty. I stopped and grabbed two dozen donuts because I knew there was still going to be family at the hospital, and I grabbed Deon a breakfast sandwich and a cup of coffee.

Just as I thought, Trina's family was still in the waiting room as well as Deon's family. All eyes were on me as I sat the donuts on the table and let Deon know they were for everybody. He sat in the chair, eyes swollen from crying.
"So are there any updates?" I asked him.
"They have to do surgery. When he hit his head, it caused his brain to swell. So he has fluid on his brain. They need to go in and put a little hole in his skull to relieve some of the pressure on his brain," Deon said.
"So when is the surgery?" I asked.
"Tomorrow morning hopefully," he said.

Deon burst in to tears. He was really scared. I blinked back my tears, because one of us had to be strong.
"I just can't stop crying," he said.
"It's OK. Go ahead and let it out," I said, rubbing his back.
"It's just a lot Rose. I have to try to hold myself together for everybody else. Then every time the doctors try to explain what's going on I have to explain it to Trina because she don't really get what they're saying... And I'm worried about my son... I don't know what I'm gonna do if I lose my son," Deon sniffled.

I hated seeing him like that! I wouldn't wish that on my worst enemy! The pain of seeing your child hurt is the worst pain in the world I think... So I just sat there and consoled him the best way that I could. There was nothing else that I could do. Once Deon got himself together, he went back to Man Man's room to check on him. I went to take a bathroom break, and to get a bite to eat from the cafeteria. Once I got back, Deon told me that he wanted to speak to me outside. I wondered what it could be about since he wanted to step outside, but I didn't put up a fuss.

"So wassup?" I asked once we were standing out front of the hospital.

"Her father pulled me to the side and said something about you kissing me before you left," Deon said.

"OK so. You're my husband. What's the issue?"

"I guess he felt like this wasn't the time or the place for it."

"What? Deon I'm grown. We are married. And it ain't like I slobbed you down and started humping on you or something. Now what you should've told him is this is the wrong time for him to be trying to pick a stupid ass argument about your wife showing affection to you."

"I know Rosie chill. I was just telling you. They just acting crazy. Trina feels some type of way because you haven't spoke to her yet either."

Now this was just unreal. Here it is, her son is hanging on to life by a thread and she was worried about me speaking to her? What?

"Deon I didn't even know she noticed I was there. She looked like she was in a whole 'nother world. I was just trying to put myself in her shoes. If one of my kids were hurt like that I wouldn't want nobody in my face at all. I would need some time to think. I was just giving her some space. That's all. I don't have a problem with Trina. To my understanding our little beef been squashed a long time ago."

"I know. You know I know. And that's what I told her. They just acting petty right now. So I just wanted to let you know what's going on. That's all."

The rest of the day I felt some type of way. The situation was too delicate for me to put people in their place though so I decided to chill for the time being. Once I got home that evening, I decided to call Aunt Lucinda and get her take on what was going on.

"I don't know what's going on. Every time I go to the hospital I get bad vibes. And I'm like... that's my husband! I'm supposed to be there. That's my stepson! Why wouldn't I be there? It's just been really crazy. I'm trying to stay in a positive mind frame though. These are only distractions. I have to stay focused on what's really important."

"That's one thing about when there is a tragedy Rose. There is a lot of displaced anger. Everybody is so wound up that anything makes them upset, even things that they usually wouldn't care about. Stuff like this brings out the worst in people," she said.

"I see," I replied.

"So do you think it's a chance they might get back together?" Aunt Lucinda asked.

Now why in the world would she ask me that? That was kind of odd to me.

"Who? Him and Trina?"

"Yes."

"No I don't think so," I responded.

"Well have you asked him?"

"No. He's going through a lot Aunt Lucy. I'm just trying to be there for him," I said.

"OK. There's nothing wrong with that. But just be careful. Sometimes these types of things make people think they belong together. Sad events bring out underlying emotions. Just keep a watchful eye Rosie. That's all I'm saying... And if it does happen don't be surprised," Aunt Lucinda replied.

"OK," was all I could say.

After I got off the phone with my Aunt, my mind began to drift a bit. Did I have something to worry about as far as Trina went? Nah. They could barely stand each other. They were co parenting. Barely. That was it. It was cool.

I tossed and turned as usual that night, and finally I decided to get up. I wasn't going to be able to sleep. So my mind went to a place of what I could do to help Deon get through this difficult time. There was nothing that my money could buy to make him feel better... So what could I do or say? I decided to do something that I hadn't done since high school. I was going to write Deon a letter. So I grabbed my journal and began to write:

Hey Deon,

Just sitting here thinking about you, and about us. I am very proud of you. You are stepping up and being the man that you are supposed to be. I know that you are scared. But just know that God is there with you. And know that I am here, and whatever you need I am willing to help. This process is going to be tough, but you are going to have to be patient and trust God. Nobody can work this out but God. Stay focused. Don't let the devil win. Don't let him distract you. When you feel a little weak or confused about what's going on, here are some bible verses for you to lean on:

HAVE FAITH

Matthew 21:22 And all things, whatsoever ye shall ask in prayer,

believing, ye shall receive.
Luke 1:37 For with God nothing shall be impossible.
Proverbs 3:5 Trust in the Lord with all thine heart; and lean not unto thine own understanding.
Hebrews 11:6 But without faith it is impossible to please him: for he that cometh to God must believe that he is, and that he is a rewarder of them that diligently seek him.
PRAY
Philippians 4:6-7 Do not be anxious about anything, but in everything by prayer and supplication with thanksgiving let your requests be made known to God. And the peace of God, which surpasses all understanding, will guard your hearts and minds in Christ Jesus.
Mark 11:24 Therefore I tell you, whatever you ask in prayer, you will receive, if you have faith.

1 Chronicles 16:11 Seek the Lord and his strength; seek his presence continually!

2 Chronicles If my people who are called by my name humble themselves, and pray and seek my face and turn from their wicked ways, then I will hear from heaven and will forgive their sin and heal their land.

GOD HEALS

James 5:14-15 Is anyone among you sick? Let him call for the elders of the church, and let them pray over him, anointing him with oil in the name of the Lord. And the prayer of faith will save the sick, and the Lord will raise him up. And if he has committed sins, he will be forgiven.

Matthew 14:14 And when Jesus went out he saw a great multitude; and He was moved with compassion for them, and healed their sick.

Psalms 107:20 He sent his word and

healed them, and delivered them from their destructions.

I pray that this may help you get through all of this. There is always light at the end of the tunnel. So look toward the sunshine. I love you, and remember... I am here whenever you need me. But most importantly, seek God and he will guide you.

I am committed to making this work Deon. We have been in each others lives for too long and we have too much at stake to just let it fall by the wayside. I love you. I want this to work. I am willing to start over with a clean slate again.

Love,
Rosie

CHAPTER 18
Love Will Make You Stupid

The next morning after I dropped the kids off, I made my way back to the hospital. Before I got there, I made a pit stop at Walmart and grabbed a card for Trina. I knew she was really going through it. A few words of encouragement might help her. I was feeling really good for some reason. I was really excited to see Deon too. Man Man was still being kept asleep by the doctors, and he had under gone the brain surgery that he needed. Things weren't looking as bad as they had been in the beginning. He still had a long way to go, but things seemed to be moving in a positive direction.

I went in to Man Man's room and Trina was sitting in the recliner staring at him. Her eyes were puffy, I could tell that she had been crying. This had to be hard for her.
"He's looking better, the swelling has went down a lot," I said to her.
"Yeah it has," she responded.

I stooped down and gave her a hug, then handed her the card.
"Thank you," she said.
"So how are you holding up?" I asked her trying to make conversation.
"The best I can. I'm trying," she answered.
"That's all you can do," I said to her.

After staying in the room for about ten minutes, I went back into to the waiting area where Deon was. He was entertaining his family, so I went and sat down.
"Hey babe," he said once he finally came over to where I was.
"Hey. Wassup?"
"Nothing. Can you do me a favor though?" he asked.
"Sure. What is it?"
"When you take my laundry home today, can you take Trina's too? She hasn't been home since Man Man's been here... Her mother brought her some stuff here but it's starting to pile up..."

What? So now I was the maid? I know that he knew I wanted to be there for him... But I hadn't said anything about her. What did I look like washing another woman's clothes? I felt my head start to hurt. Then I asked myself... What would Jesus do?

"Yeah no problem," I lied.

It definitely was a problem. But I was so busy trying to show Deon that I was down for him that I was willing to do something that I really had a problem with. I plastered a fake smile on my face until it was time for me to go get the kids from school. I carried the bag of laundry to my car and threw it into the trunk then slammed it. I got in the car and then got back out. I went back to the trunk and opened it. For some reason I wanted to know what was in the bag. So I fished through it and saw a few of Deon's sweat pants, then what had to be Trina's pajama pants. I pulled my hand from the bag and a pair of her drawers fell out of the bag onto the ground. I can't even call them panties. That's how nasty they were. What in the world? How could a woman walk around with all those nasty stains in the seat of underwear? Brown and red. That's all I can say. Brown and red. I got a pen from my car and used it to lift those nasty things off the ground and flung them back into the bag. I slammed the trunk then got back in my car and doused my hands with the hand sanitizer that I kept in the glove compartment. I had a momentary flash back of the nastiness I had just saw, which caused me to gag a little. Then I thought back to the conversation that I had with Aunt Lucy. Did I think Deon would go back to her? Hell no. Not with those nasty drawers.

I decided to drop the laundry to a wash dry and fold service. It was no way I was going to make the mistake of touching that stuff again. I went and grabbed the kids, then dropped them off to Rochelle. Next, I went to pick up the laundry and then I headed back to the hospital.

I stepped off of the elevator and walked up the hall, laundry bag in tow. I bent the corner, and there was Deon talking to some woman who I had never seen before. Deon's back was to me, so he didn't even know I was there. Something wasn't right, I could feel it. So I stepped back behind the corner so I could eavesdrop on their little meeting.

"So you couldn't call me and tell me that Deonte was hurt? I had to hear about it on the news? Really?" she probed.

"I mean what did I have to call you for? You been acting like you ain't have no rap anyway. You won't let me see my son-"

"You call for everything else! You find a way to call for everything else! You are selfish! This is why I can't deal with you! This is why I don't want you around my son!" she screamed interrupting Deon.

OK. So I had heard enough. It was time for me to make my presence known and to find out what the hell was going on here. I stepped from around the corner so that I was in plain sight.

"Who are you?" I butted in.

She looked at me as if I were a disease. So in turn, I stared right through her. If she wanted to have a staring contest, then we could do this all day.

"Why don't you ask him? Who am I Deon?" she asked with a smirk on her face.

"Come on yall, this ain't the time for this," Deon tried to cop out.

"Oh yes it is. Who is she?" I asked.

Deon had the "oh shit I'm caught," face that I knew all too well. And that look made my stomach drop. This man had entirely too much stuff with him. What was he going to say now?

"Let me talk to you outside," he said.

"No. I don't need you trying to downplay the situation. Whatever you can say outside you can say right here."

Deon looked down at the floor. At this point I was beyond pissed. All he had to do was man up and be honest. FOR ONCE.

"Well since the cat seems to have gotten a hold of his tongue, let me enlighten you. My name is Phoenix. I am the mother of Deon's oldest son... Deon Jr.," she said proudly.

I was confused. I thought Mocha was Deon's mother. Was my mind playing tricks on me? Did I hear her right? Her

voice interrupted my thoughts.
"I guess your husband hasn't told you anything about my son. But your husband is a liar, so I'm not surprised. So the next time you approach somebody maybe you should think twice and get the facts first."
"First of all bitch don't play with me. I will slap the shit out of you," I said dropping my purse to the floor.
"It's no need for you to get hostile. I don't want him. Now does he want me? That's the question you should be asking. I don't want to fight you. I have no reason to. I have no ties to him besides my son, and I don't even need him to do anything for him so I'm good," Phoenix said adjusting her purse strap on her shoulder.
"So why are you here?" I asked her.
"To see about Deonte'. I mean he is my son's brother. And I do have a relationship with him and his mother as well," she said tucking her red hair behind her ear. "Look like I said before I don't want Deon. I haven't done anything thing with him since my son was conceived... And that was like thirteen years ago."
"What are you talking about?" I asked.
"Phoenix please let me talk to her," Deon finally spoke.
"OK. I need to go in here and see Deonte' anyway," Phoenix said before walking away.
"Deon what the fuck is going on?" I asked him through my clenched jaw.
"Rose please come outside with me so we can talk," he answered back.
   The elevator ride was super tense. I wanted to knock his teeth out right then and there, but then he wouldn't be able to tell me what the hell was going on. I marched off the elevator and made a B-line for front exit of the hospital. Once we got outside, I got right to it.
"I don't want no beating around the bush. Just tell me what the hell is going on so I can get out the dark."
"OK. So... Phoenix was Trina's room mate in college... I had a threesome with Trina and Phoenix... and Phoenix got pregnant... she said she wasn't going to keep the baby but she

did... So that's what she was talking about when she said she has my oldest son... Deonte' is really my second son. Deon Jr. by Phoenix is my first," Deon said letting out a deep breath.

Oh no this nigga didn't just let out a sigh of relief after dropping that bomb on me! He must've lost his mind! Here I was, coming to check on my stepson who I thought was the oldest and now I had to find out about another son who I had never heard about? Not to mention the bomb that had been dropped on me three years ago when Mocha left the other Deon Jr. at my front door! How much was I supposed to take? "WHAT? SO YOU DIDN'T THINK THAT I SHOULD KNOW THAT? DEON WHAT THE FUCK IS WRONG WITH YOU? WHY DO I HAVE TO KEEP FINDING THINGS OUT YOU? THIS MARRIAGE HAS BEEN NOTHING BUT SECRETS AND LIES!" I screamed.
"Rose please don't scream out here people are going to he-"
"WHAT? HEAR HOW MUCH OF A LIAR YOU ARE? I DON'T CARE WHO HEARS ME! I'M DONE KEEPING UP THIS MAKE PRETEND FAIRYTALE OF A MARRIAGE THAT WE DON'T HAVE DEON! I'M SICK OF IT! THIS DOESN'T MAKE ANY SENSE! I HAVE BEEN GOOD TO YOU! I HAVE STUCK BY YOU! AND YOU CONTINUOUSLY MAKE ME LOOK LIKE A FOOL!"
"Rose I'm sorry," Deon lied.
"No you're not. You're not sorry. No. You know what? You are sorry. You are a sorry excuse for a man. Instead of being a man and owning up to your shit you wait until you are backed into a corner and then you tell the truth. That's not right. And what did she mean you find a way to contact her about everything else? All this time we have been married I have never seen your son so what could you possibly be contacting her about?" I quizzed.
"Rosie she's just mad that I didn't call her and tell her about Deonte'."
"Deon... Whatever. I can't believe not one word that comes out of your mouth. This is so fucked up. Because obviously she knows Deonte'... which means she has some type of

relationship with him and Trina, and still nobody bothered to tell me anything... I don't have anything else to say to you right now. Just leave me alone," I said before leaving Deon standing where he was.

I stomped to my car and got in. I fished around in my purse for my lip gloss. I needed some type of continual motion to calm me down. The letter that I wrote Deon brush against my hand, which annoyed me even more. I wanted to rip it in to a thousand little pieces, but it wouldn't change a thing. Even though I was so pissed with him... I still wanted him. I just wanted him to do right. No woman wants to have to start all the way over. We just want the man that we have dedicated our all to, the one that we have invested all our time in... All we want is for that man to realize the gem that they have and to treat us as such. Why is that so hard to do?

CHAPTER 19
The Straw That Broke The Camel's Back

Deon blew my phone up for the next few days, but I didn't bother to answer. I wasn't ready to take him back yet. I wanted to scare him a little bit I guess. Maybe, just maybe we could put all the messiness behind us and move the hell on. Like REALLY move on. I was so tired of the back and forth. That was for boyfriends and girlfriends, not for husbands and wives. I know that no marriage is perfect, but we were doing too much. It was time to get this thing right.

So on the fourth day, I finally decided to answer when he called. Enough was enough. I needed to hear his voice. Say what you want, I loved him.

"Rosie I apologize for not being honest with you. The situation was just so fucked up I ain't even know how to explain it," Deon whined.

"Easy. The same way you explained it when you had no choice. Look Deon, we're too old for this. And I don't' know about you, but I'm tired of the back and forth. I just want us to be together and raise these kids and be happy. I don't want to hear excuses for why you lied... I just want you to own up to it and let me know what it is that you're gonna do to make our situation better. I can't do nothing with excuses," I responded calmly.

"OK."

"OK what? So what are you going to do differently to make sure that we don't have to keep going through this?"

"I just have to be honest with you Rose. I can't keep things from you. I have to be honest," he said.

"Even deeper than that Deon... You have to stop putting yourself in situations where you even feel like you're gonna have to lie about it. You are married. That means you have to be faithful. It's that simple. You have to exercise some sort of self control," I said.

"You're right," Deon said.

"Is this what you really want?" I asked him.

"What?"

"This marriage. Is this really what you want? Because I'm not in the business of holding hostages. If you want to be single and do your thing just let me know."

"Yes I want this marriage you know that," Deon snapped.

"No I don't know that's why I'm asking you. Your actions this past year have not reflected you wanting this marriage. And you begging to come back when I put you out doesn't mean that you want this marriage. That's just your automatic response when you see us going down the drain," I said.

"Rosie. I want this marriage. I want you. I want our family. That's all."

"And what about Rochelle?" I asked.

That's right. I had to ask the million dollar question. There was no way that I was even going to be able to think of patching things up with Deon unless I got some sort of explanation about what that was all about. He wasn't going to just move back in like nothing happened.

"Do we have to talk about that?" he whined some more.

"Yes we do have to talk about *that*. That's the original elephant in the room. I'm not about to allow you to come back if you can't even tell me why you tried to cheat on me with my best friend. I think I'm worth an explanation... I need to know something. Why did you do it? Like what would make you say, okay Imma gonna try my hand with my wife's best friend today? How do you think I feel knowing that I'm gonna have to have yall two in the same room together again one day? How am I supposed to be able to trust you Deon when you continually make decisions that result in me not trusting you? Do you understand what I'm saying to you?"

"Yes. I get it. I do. I haven't been doing things the right way. I wish I could give you an explanation as to why I did it but I really don't know. No reason is going to be a good enough reason for what I did."

I wanted to huff and puff some more, but it was getting late... Well not late, but too late to be arguing. Ten thirty at night the only thing that should be going on is sleeping, rolling around in the sheets with somebody, or relaxing getting mentally prepared for the next day... Not arguing or scolding somebody.

"I'm just done fighting Deon. I'm doing a lot right now and now I gotta figure out if I'm going to go through with the reality show," I rambled.

"Reality show? What reality show?" Deon probed.

"Oh yeah... I never got around to talking to you about it. Well VH1 is trying to get me to sign on a reality show with them... I haven't given them back a definite answer yet," I replied.

"So we're gonna do it right?" Deon continued to pry.

"Is that something you would want to do? I never said anything to you about it because I was kind of skeptical about how you would feel," I said.

"Yeah! I'll do it."

I was really shocked. Since when did Deon start being into that type of stuff? He always called those type of shows phoney when I watched them at home.

"I want you back home," I cooed.

"Can I come back home?" Deon teased.

"Stop playin'..."

"OK then. You know I'm coming back."

"I love you."

"I love you too."

I wanted to stay on the phone all night like we did when we first got married and he was on the road. But things were nothing like they were back then. I had been working all day and I was dead tired. But my mind automatically went back to business.

"Well I'll make the phone call in the morning and I'll set up another meeting for all of us."

"That's cool," Deon said.

"So look, I need to check behind the kids and make sure they got everything ready for tomorrow, then I need to get some rest. It would be nice if you could come here tonight," I purred.

"You know I wish I could babe. But I gotta be here just in case something happens."

I knew he was going to say that.

"Okay... I'll be up there the first thing in the morning. Plus I got something to give you," I said.
"What is it?"
"A letter."
"A letter?"
"Yeah it ain't nothing bad just something nice I want you to read," I responded.
"That's cool. But go ahead to work tomorrow. Just come up to here after you're done," Deon instructed.

I was confused. I was ready to get back to the normal routine. Staying at the hospital during the day, picking the kids up from school and daycare, taking them home, feeding them dinner and getting them in bed... Then down the hospital for a couple hours, then back home to go to bed, then up the next morning to do it all over again.
"Why?" I asked.
"You need to stay focused on your career. I know you are concerned. But I'll make sure I keep you updated while you're at work," he replied.
"But I told you I had that taken care of. Lexi was patching me through to any calls I absolutely had to take. I take care of any paperwork I have at night before I go to bed. I still make time to drop into the daycare... I really have it under control. I need to be there for you," I said.
"I know. But I know how you love to be hands on. You don't have to rearrange everything."

The ending of the conversation is still fuzzy because I had totally zoned out. I tossed and turned after we ended the call and I got in bed. I missed my husband. And I missed Deonte' too. I needed to see them now. So I hopped out of the bed and threw on a white tank top and some gray yoga pants. I slipped on a pair of Jordans and didn't even bother tying the shoe strings. I needed to see his face even if it were a few minutes. I wrote a note and stuck it on Miracle's door just in case she woke up in the middle of the night. Summer was in Miracle's bed, so she was good. Lil Franko slept like a rock so he was good too. I set the alarm and hopped in my car. I couldn't wait to wrap my arms around him. That's all I needed. I wouldn't be long. I just wanted to pop in and pop out.

After parking the car I made my way inside the hospital. I went in and passed the security guard's desk. It was the same one that was there every Wednesday night. She knew who I was so she didn't bother telling me that visiting hours had been over. I bent that same corner where I had walked in on Deon and his estranged baby mama. I shook my head at the memory and continued on to Man Man's room and walked in. My heart sank. I stood there in total disbelief. My husband had his lips pressed up against his ex wife's lips.

I dropped the letter that I had folded in between ten other sheets of paper on the floor. I could tell that I had startled them. They pulled away from each other and I said nothing. I left right back out of the room. As bad as I wanted to tear that whole room apart, I wasn't going to do it. I wasn't going to make a fool of myself anymore than Deon had already done for me. So I sacheted down the hall as if it were a runway. My eyes blurred with tears but I blinked them away. It was time for me to leave this whole thing where it needed to be. In the trash. I had been stupid long enough.

I could hear footsteps behind me and I already knew who it was. I just kept on strutting pretending as if I didn't know that he was trying to catch up to me to plead his case. I got on the elevator and pushed the close doors button in hopes to shut him out, but to my dismay... No luck. He stuck his hands between the doors before they could shut all the way which caused them to reopen.

"Rosie just let me explain," Deon said.

"I'm tired of this Deon! I keep giving you chance ,after chance, after chance ,after chance, after chance! And every time I give you another chance you shit on me every time I can't do this anymore! I'm done! Be with her! Go ahead and be with her I can't do this anymore! I'm not doing this anymore you have hurt me too many times I can't do this," I cried.

"But what about the show?" Deon asked.

"The show? What about the show? I just told you that our

marriage is over for good, and all you are concerned about is a dumb ass reality show? Are you serious? Just when I think you have done the worst you come right back with something even worse! Just leave me the fuck alone!"

I looked over at the buttons and realized that I hadn't pressed any of the numbers, so we were sitting still. I pressed the number one with the star beside it, an Deon grabbed my hand.

"I said get the fuck off of me," I yelled.

All of a sudden I went into full attack mode. I kicked and punched him as hard as I could. He finally grabbed a hold of me, and the elevator doors popped open.

"Don't make a scene, the security guard is right there," he whispered in my ear.

"I said get off of my you lying bitch!" I screamed.

The security guard looked up from her phone, and Deon let me go.

"What's going on?" she asked coming from behind her desk.

"Nothing," Deon lied like he always did.

I said nothing. I stormed through the lobby and out of the glass double doors all the way to my car without looking back. No more. I was done. No more.

Riding home with the recent events rewinding in my head continuously was nothing short of torture. God had shown me over and over again and I had chosen to either ignore his signs, or forgive them. No more. I deserved better. I was worth much more than the levels that this marriage was causing me to stoop to. No more. I didn't need him. Sure I would miss him, but eventually I would get over it. I had survived after my relationships with Franko, Marlon, and Ra-Ra… So this situation with Deon wasn't going to kill me either. People got divorces all the time and somehow, they survived too. It was no reason to go hide under a rock though. I was going to hold my head high, and rise above that whole situation.

By the time I got home, my whole way of thinking had shifted. I was pissed. I was hurt. I was aggravated. I was irritated. I was frustrated. I was sexually frustrated. I wanted to get even. I was tired of being the bigger person. I was tired of letting Deon do all types of things and being the super passive wife. I was tired of thinking, "what would Jesus do?" At that moment I wanted to do what Rose wanted to do. I picked up the phone and dialed.

CHAPTER 20
The Best Way To Get Over the Other One... Is With Another One

"Well hey there, I haven't heard from you in a while," Brent answered.

"Yea. I know," I replied as I walked through the front door.

"OK. Well I'm glad to hear from you. I heard about what happened to Deon's son. How is he doing?"

"He's doing better. It's going to be a process, but he's gonna pull through."

"Well that's good to hear. So how is Deon making out? I mean how is he handling things?" Brent continued to pry.

I wanted to blurt out how much of a lying mutt Deon was, but I decided against it. Instead I kept it short and uninteresting.

"He's fine," I replied.

I guess Brent could sense the irritation in my voice because he quickly changed the subject.

"OK... So what have you been up to Ms. Busy Lady? What new business ventures have you signed on to?"

"Just waiting for the ink to dry on this deal with this lingerie company. Other than that just keeping up with the normal stuff... The daycare... The nanny placement business... Setting up a few things for Leandro... And keeping Violet booked with maternity work... Oh and of course the shoe line is still popping," I said.

"OK. OK. That's what I like to hear. Making moves as always."

"Yea. I don't have anything else to do," I said.

"What is that supposed to mean?" Brent inquired.

"Nothing," I replied.

"It seems like something is on your mind, do you want to talk about it?"

I hesitated for a second, "no."

"I can't help but to think that you aren't being honest," Brent said. "Look. How about I take you out. Let me show you a good time."

I hadn't been out on a date with Deon in so long that the

offer from Brent sounded awesome. But I couldn't do that. I couldn't be seen in public with Brent. That just wouldn't look good.

"Um... No... I.. I can't," I stammered.

"Oh I see. Still worried about how things will look huh? Well.... I'll do you one better. Come on over to my house. I'm a low key guy, no paparazzi, no stalkers," Brent chuckled.

"I don't know..."

"Rose. We're both adults here. I'm not trying to pressure you though. You just sound like you need to talk, like you need to get some things off your chest. I prefer face to face conversations over phone chatting any day. When you're ready to leave you can. I'm not gonna hold you hostage."

There was something about Brent's tone that was so reassuring. I did want some company. But I didn't want him at my house. So maybe going over to his house for a few would be OK.

I finally caved in. "Alright. Give me about an hour and a half."

"OK. Cool. I'll text you the address," Brent said.

"Alright. See you in a few," I said before hanging up.

Before I could get up from the sofa, the text was coming through. Damn. Brent lived in Shady side Maryland. He had told me that in a previous conversation. And I lived in Waldorf. That was almost an hour drive without traffic. Damn. I needed to get a move on. But I couldn't leave the kids home alone all night! Damn, damn, damn. Then the light bulb went off.

"Ro, I need you to come stay with the kids,"I said into the phone.

"Well hello to you too," her voice cracked.

"Oh hey. Sorry. Oh my goodness you were sleep weren't you? My bad. Nevermind."

"No wait Rosie what's going on?"

"Nothing I just wanted to stay out for a little while," I answered.

"At the hospital?" Rochelle asked

Her comment struck a nerve. But she didn't know what

had just happened. I shook it off.
"No... No. I'm done with Deon."
"What?"
"It's a long story... Not for right now. But anyway I wanna go over to Brent's house."
"Oh my word," Rochelle laughed.
"Rochelle come on now don't do that-"
"I'm not judging just happy you about to get some new new," she continued to laugh.
"Who said anything was going to happen?" I asked.
"You, when you decided to go visit him this time of morning," Rochelle laughed again. "Let me brush my teeth and slip something on. Give me a couple minutes."
"Okay thanks."
"No problem."

  Once Rochelle got to the house, I was on my way. The smell of my Nicki Minaj perfume intoxicated my own nostrils. I was nervous though. I really didn't know what to expect. When I pulled up to his house, I was amazed at how open it was. No security gate or anything. He must've trusted that no one would come stalk him. I thought that too until Mocha showed up on my doorstep. Anyway, I parked in the drive way and walked up to the door. Before I could even knock, Brent was opening the door. That's right... He was anticipating this pretty red thang switching up to his doorstep. Ha!

  I walked inside and he asked me to remove my shoes. I wasn't offended. He had snow white carpet, and it was spotless. I kicked off my black red bottoms that he had sent to my office. Brent looked down at the shoes and smiled. He picked them up and walked toward the stairs.
"Where are we going?' I asked.
"Upstairs... Unless you want to stay down here. But I have everything set up upstairs."
"Set up?" I asked.
"Yeah. Some fruit... I remember you saying you were dieting... And some wine... I got Skinny Girl wine for you... Just some stuff so you can relax and vent," he said with a smile.

"OK," I replied.

I followed him up the marble staircase, and down the hall to his room. We passed four bedrooms before getting to his and once we stepped inside and it was absolutely gorgeous. Well actually kind of sexy. He had an all black bedroom. Black leather headboard. Black sheets. Black dresser and nightstand. A black leather loveseat. Plus a black coffee table situated in front of it. There was an enormous flat screen mounted to the wall, and a fish tank mounted into one of the other walls. There was a crystal chandelier hanging in the center of the room, with mirrors lining the whole ceiling. A vain little thing he was. Well he definitely wasn't little, I'm speaking figuratively. Anyway I looked to the right of me and to my surprise there it was. A pole. I kind of smirked. I had always wanted to get a pole for my bedroom at home, but Deon didn't want me to. Go figure.

Brent sat down on the loveseat and patted his hand beside him, signaling me to come and take a seat. I decided to be obedient, and sat down. Brent poured me a glass of wine and I took a big gulp as soon as he finished pouring. He laughed and I didn't care. With the night that I had, I needed the whole bottle.

"So what's the matter?" Brent asked.

"Nothing."

"So you like lying huh?"

"No."

"Well talk to me. What's the problem?"

I didn't know whether I should tell Brent what happened or not. I didn't want him to know that the only reason I had decided to come over there was because Deon had betrayed me. AGAIN. So I decided not to go into detail.

"Just realizing that my marriage is over," I said.

"Well I thought you already knew that," Brent said chewing a grape.

"I did."

"So what's the problem?"

"It's really starting to sink in I guess."

Damn this dude was like a news reporter. He wanted the

scoop, the whole scoop, and nothing but the scoop! Ha! But he could keep on wanting, because I wasn't about to cry on his shoulder about my husband cheating on me.

"These don't bother you?" Brent asked brushing my bangs away from my eyes with his fingers.

"No," I said brushing them back into place.

"Loosen up you seem tense," Brent said.

"I'm not tense," I said.

"OK if you say so," he replied pouring me another glass of wine.

I grabbed a strawberry from the dish on the coffee table and took a bite. Then I drank my second glass of wine straight down. I needed to be numb. I sat down my glass and when I looked up, Brent was staring me dead in my face.

"Can I help you?" I asked playfully.

"Yes. Can you tell me why you are so beautiful?"

Oh no. Not the compliments. I was on the verge of tipsy so I didn't need any compliments. I changed the subject.

"Your room is really nice," I said.

"You like it?" he asked.

"Yup. I love black."

"Me too," Brent said.

He picked up the wine bottle and poured me another glass.

"Are you trying to get me drunk?" I inquired.

"Nah. Just trying to relax you a little bit. I feel like you need to relax. You're a busy woman. You deserve to kick back a little," Brent replied.

Well didn't he know all the right things to say? This man was just as smooth as he wanted to be... I smiled and took a drink from my glass. We talked for a few about a little bit of everything... My businesses... My goals for the future... His goals for the future... His family... My crazy family (Violet)... It was nice talking to him. He was easy to talk to, and he seemed to really pay attention when I talked. I liked that.

I excused myself and stepped out on the balcony to get some fresh air. I was beginning to feel rather warm from all that wine that I had drank. I looked off into the darkness and took a deep breath. The stars were like little specs of diamond dust sprinkled across the sky. Well maybe it was the wine. But at any rate, the atmosphere was a calming one. I leaned forward against the railing that encased the balcony and the next thing I knew I felt a tingle on my neck.

"Are you gonna come back inside with me?" Brent whispered in my ear.

My heart rate picked up speed. It had been a while since I had someone in my intimate space. But I had to hold it together. I couldn't show him that he was making me melt like butter.

"Yeah. In a few," I said coolly.

Brent wrapped his hands around my waist from behind. I thought my eyes were gonna pop out of my head. Good thing he couldn't see my facial expression or he might have thought I was crazy.

"Am I too close?" he asked.

"No. You're fine."

Brent slid his hands up my shirt and caressed my breasts. I was hoping that he couldn't feel the vibration of my heart beat while he was fondling me.

"What about now?" he teased.

I was on to the game he was playing. Every time I said no he was going to take it a step further. So I had a dilemma. What should my answer be? Yes or no?

"No," I whispered.

And just like clock work, he took it a step further. He spun me around and slid his hands down my back to my butt. He squeezed it gently, and I thought I was going to pass out any second. I guess he was done playing games because at this point he was going in for the kill. He looked me straight in my eyes and I looked away. This was too much. He lightly nudged my chin so that I was face to face with him again.

"Look at me," he said.

I didn't know what to say, so I just looked at him like he had told me to do.

"You want me to fuck your brains out don't you?" he asked.
"Yes," I answered him.

Wait did I just say that? Yes I did. I felt so embarrassed. I didn't know why, but I did. I guess because Deon didn't talk like that. Not saying that I didn't like I because I did. Itwas just new. In the midst of me obsessing in my head over the fact that I had just outwardly admitted that I wanted him to tear me apart, he kissed me. And not just a peck. I'm talking lip smacking and tongue action. All that. And he knew what he was doing. Didn't leave all around my mouth wet either. So anyway, he picked me up and threw me over his shoulder. I giggled a little and he slapped me on my butt. How did he know I liked that? Ha! He tossed me on the bed and lifted my legs in the air.

"Oh yeah you wanted me in there anyway. No panties huh?"

I blushed a tiny bit. He was right. I had plans on doing the do when I made the initial phone call to him earlier that night. I wasn't going to admit to it though. Brent let my legs down gently then he took off his shirt. And let me tell you... That man's body was on point do you hear me? He pressed his body against mine, then he whispered in my ear again.

"So when is the last time he made you have an orgasm?" Brent asked.
"Why are you asking me that?"
"Because I want to know," he said
"Why?" I asked again.
"Because I want to make you have as many as you want... Whenever you want."
"Well you can start now," I said.

And without me giving him any further direction, he did just that. He put his head underneath my dress and made me experience the most intense orgasm that I had ever felt in my life. And he didn't stop. He wouldn't stop. After the fourth one I was begging him to stop. All my limbs felt like they were two hundred pounds each. I couldn't move.
"Stop," I moaned.
"Shut up. Don't tell me to stop," Brent commanded.

Brent was something I had never experienced before. I thought Deon was the best at one time. However, my time in the sack with Mr. Brent changed all that. He was super aggressive. He was experienced. He knew how to control a woman's body and I loved that. Brent had stamina too, which was an extra check plus. We went at it all night... Changing positions and just being plain ole freaky. Gosh he was nasty. And he talked a lot of trash too. He wrapped my hair around his hand while he was behind me and yanked my head back. Then he bit me on my right butt cheek. I thought I would die. I know that people would say that this was wrong... But it felt so right! Brent made me feel so young again.. So free...
"Do you like that?" he probed.
"Yes," I squealed.
"Do you want me to do it again?"
"Yes."
"Yes what?"
"Yes Daddy."
"Do you want me to stop?"
"Noooo..."
"Say please..."
"Please don't stop."

Oh my gosh! I couldn't believe my own ears! Or eyes! On a scale of one to ten Brent was a seven thousand thirty two! Where had he been all my life? And just when I thought it couldn't get any better, he pulled away and got up from the bed. I sat up straight to see what he was doing. I'm not sure how much time had elapsed but I was a bit annoyed because I was truly enjoying myself. Brent slid his hand between the mattress and pulled out a few bands. He picked up the remote to his sound system and the next thing I knew "Pour It Up" was playing. He grabbed my shoes from the floor and handed them to me, then looked over at the pole that was positioned in the corner of the room. I thought about playing the innocent role and declining. But hell, I had been open for I don't know how long already... So there was no point in stopping now.

Brent took a seat in the black leather recliner that was

across from the pole. I slipped on my shoes and got right to it like I had never retired. I guess it was like riding a bike, because everything came right back. The movements of my body were just as fluid as they had been six years ago. And Brent showed his satisfaction for sure. Money rained all over me and I was in my zone. Once my performance was over, we brought the night to a close on the balcony all over each other like it was our last time together. After we were done and completely worn out, we dragged ourselves back inside and got in bed.

 My eyes popped open and I scrambled for my phone. I looked at my home screen and I wanted to scream! It was six thirty in the morning! I had to get home and get my kids to school! I jumped up and started throwing my clothes on. I had to get out of there. Fast.

"Where you going?" Brent ask groggily.
"I gotta get home. Motherhood calls," I said.
"Ok. I get you. Can I see you later?"
"I'm not sure. Maybe."

 I rushed into his master bathroom to pee. Damn! I didn't bring my toothbrush.
"There are extra toothbrushes in the medicine cabinet," Brent called out to me.
"Thanks," I said while washing my hands.

 I grabbed a toothbrush and began to brush my teeth. I did a mental scan of what I had to do that day. I had to drop the Porsche off to get detailed and I needed to go to the grocery store. Plus I needed make sure that Lexi had booked the flight to Atlanta for V and I. She had a maternity on Friday.
"You know you're mine now right?" Brent called out to me again.

 I spit the excess toothpaste in the sink. What in the world? I know we had a good night but damn! He was ready to cuff me already! I wasn't with it. Well I was, but I couldn't. It just wouldn't look right. I had to try to slow roll it for real. So I didn't answer him. Instead, I finished brushing my teeth then hurried out of the bathroom. I gathered my purse and put my

shoes on.
I'm gonna kiss you right in your mouth right in front of him," Brent said.

Whoa now. Now he was really pushing it. I felt the fire works just as well as he did. But it was just too soon for the public announcement. I wasn't even sure if being with him was what I really wanted. The sex was magnificent, no lie. But... that wasn't enough to base a whole relationship on. Or was it?
"Nooo... No you're not," I stammered.
"See. I told you. You're not over him."
"Yes I am. Yes. Yes I am.. It's just... I'm not ready for the back lash of it. I just don't feel like dealing with the rumors and all the tabloids," I confessed.
"OK fine. If you're not ready then I won't pressure you. We know what we know and that's cool with me."

Brent offered to walk me out to my car and I declined. He would just slow me down with all the mushiness. I really had to get home and get my day started.
"You're forgetting something," Brent said pointing to the money scattered on the floor.
"That's okay. I don't need your money," I said before I exited.

CHAPTER 21
Everything Happens For A Reason

"Hey V wassup?" I said as I pulled out of Brent's driveway.

I wondered what her pregnant behind was calling me for this early in the morning for. Whatever it was, she had to make it quick because I needed to call Rochelle and let her know I was on my way.

"My water broke," Violet said in a panic.

"What?"

This couldn't be happening she was only twenty four weeks. I was terrified. This wasn't good at all.

"My water broke!"

"Are you sure?"

"Yes my my pants are wet and not like pee I couldn't stop it," she cried.

"Are you home?" I asked.

"Yes!"

"OK. Keep the phone by you I'm going to call an ambulance."

I called an ambulance immediately after I hung up the phone with Violet, then dialed Rochelle's number.

"Hey girl! So how was your night?" Rochelle asked as soon as the call connected.

I totally dismissed her question. My night of lust wasn't important right now. I had to get to Violet.

"Violet said her water broke. I'm on my way to D.C. Now. Can you please make sure the kids get to school? I'll call my driver and have him pick up Miracle and Franko. But Summer is going to need to be dropped off."

"Her water broke? Already?" Rochelle asked.

"Yea that's what she said. I sent an ambulance over there and I'm gonna meet them at the hospital."

"Wow. Well yeah I already had plans on taking everybody to school. I thought you might decide to sleep in at Brent's," Rochelle said.

"Oh OK. Well no I was actually on my way there until V called. But thank you so much I really appreciate it," I said.

"No problem. Just make sure you keep me posted on what's

going on."

I got to the hospital and Violet was sitting up in the bed on her phone. She looked scared. Her eyes and the tip of her nose were red. Gosh I didn't like seeing her upset. It didn't matter that I had told her not to do this in the first place. She was still my baby sister. I looked over at the monitors that kept track of the baby's heat rate, and Violets contractions.

"I'm at the hospital. I'm about to have the baby. You need to hurry up and get here before you miss it," she said into the phone.

I didn't say a word. If calling the man who impregnated her to tell him that she was about to have a baby that he cared nothing about was going to make her feel better, then that was her business. I knew that deep down she knew he wasn't coming. Violet looked up at me as she hung up the phone.

"I'm having him today. I'm already dilated six centimeters."

"Oh wow. You didn't know you were in labor?"

"Not really. I felt pain. But I don't know. I just thought it was too early. People talk about those Braxton Hicks things all the time so... I didn't know," Violet said.

"So what about and epidural? You getting one?"

"Nah. I heard all that medicine can make your baby groggy when it comes out. I'm good."

Wow. So it was real. My first nephew would come into the world on that day for sure. I called Lexi. She had already booked the flight. I gave her instructions to cancel it and to call the photographer in Atlanta to let him know that Violet would be delivering that day, so the whole maternity piece was shot. After I got off the phone, I sat down in the chair beside her. There was an awkward silence so I thought it was only right to make some conversation.

"So did you decide on what you're gonna name him?" I asked.

Violet sat straight up and grabbed the bed rail. She was having a contraction. Seeing how her body tensed up reminded me of the last time I was in labor. Once the contraction subsided, she laid back against her pillow.

"Yup. I'm gonna name him after his father," she said.

But why though? I didn't say it but I damn sure was thinking it. Why was she so interested in showing any type of respect to that no good piece of shit? I just couldn't understand it. I didn't know what it was going to take for her to get the picture. Before I could change the subject the phone rang. It was my aunt. I called her when I was on my way to the hospital but she didn't answer. I was glad she called back before the baby was born. I wanted to keep her in the loop.
"Hey Aunt Lucinda," I answered.
"Good morning. I missed your call you know I have my morning prayer and worship before I start my day," she said.
"Oh yea, that's right. I forgot."
"What wrong? You don't usually call me that early."
"Yeah... I don't. But I was calling to tell you that Violet is in the hospital... I'm here with her. She's gonna have the baby today."
"Today? It's too early ain't it?" Aunt Lucy asked.
"Yes it's early."
"Well where is she? Can she talk? Let me speak to her," she said.
"OK. Hold on one second she's having a contraction."

I held my phone against my chest while I watched Violet endure the pain. Once she relaxed again, I handed her the phone. Violet kept her answers very short, I could tell that she was very irritated now. And I hoped that my aunt didn't ask her the million dollar question.
"I don't know Aunt Lucy he's not here," Violet rolled her eyes.

There it was. I had a feeling she was going to ask her where her deadbeat baby daddy was. Violet tossed the phone onto the bed and grabbed onto the rails again.
"I feel something Rosie I think I need to push!"
"Oh my God!" I screamed.

I ran out into the hallway and screamed for a nurse to come and help her. The team of nurses ran in and the doctor came in behind them. The rest of it was a blur. All I remember is the doctor saying the baby's heart rate was dropping... Violet pushed and the baby literally fell out into the doctor's hands. He was tiny. I mean really frail. And he didn't make a sound.

"Is he okay? Is he okay?" Violet cried over and over.

No one would answer her though. The whole team was in the corner working on him frantically. But there was no use. He was already gone. After about five minutes of trying to get him to breathe, one of the nurses came over to Violet's side. "I'm so sorry. We did the best that we could. He didn't make it." "Nooooooo!!!!!!!!!" Violet screamed.

The sound was blood curdling. All I could do was grab her and hold her as tight as I could. I couldn't imagine her pain. She was so attached to that baby from the very beginning. Every time she screamed I felt a pain in my stomach. This was awful. The thought of that trifling ass Young Bread flashed in my mind, and I got angry. My little sister was in the hospital going through hell over the loss of a baby that he put in her... And he was no where to be found. I thought about how good it would make me feel to have somebody just erase him from this planet. He wasn't good for nothing anyway. He was ugly, he couldn't rap, he was a fraud... He was useless. So why not just put him out of his misery and keep him away from my sister for good?

Then reality set in. The person who set up the hit got just as much time as the person that actually did it. I never wanted to go back to jail. NEVER. I couldn't be away from my children. And if something happened to that dummy, my sister would probably drop dead. She was still in love with him. She wouldn't be happy that he was gone. And to top it all off... Who was I to determine if somebody should live or die? I'm not God. That wasn't my place. I had to push those crazy thoughts out of my head just as fast as they had entered.

Violet had calmed down a little, and by this time they had the baby cleaned up and swaddled with a little tiny blue knitted hat on. I can't even say that he was cute, he just looked like a baby. He was way too small to be cute. But he was precious. And he had a lot of hair. They gave him to Violet to hold, and she cried the whole time. And just when I thought she had calmed down, she flipped.

"Look at my baby! Yall killed my baby! I hate yall! Get away from me! Get out! Get away from my baby!" Violet screamed.

This was a situation where I felt like I had no control at all. I didn't know what to do. Violet was hysterical. And when it came time for them to take the baby, she got even worse. She eventually quieted down, but not completely. She whimpered and whined for the rest of the day. At some point, I thought she needed to hear something that made a little sense.

"God's timing is perfect V. You have to believe that. You will have another child. And this time it will be a better situation and you won't have to chase the father around to be there either. I don't know how it feels to lose a child... but I do know what loss feels like. It doesn't feel good. And it takes time to get past it. But once you get past it, you'll have a testimony. You'll be able to help someone else with your experience," I said.

"I don't want to hear that... I just want my baby. Please... Just leave me alone," she said rolling over on her side.

"OK," was all I could manage to say.

The following week, V decided that she wanted to funeralize her son. So nobody went against her wishes. She planned a very elaborate funeral. His casket was closed and it was the tiniest casket that I had ever seen. I didn't even know that they made them that little. Aunt Lucinda came up from Virginia and of course I was there with my crew. The sperm donor of the baby didn't show up and I wasn't surprised. I was glad he didn't come. He didn't deserve to be there. V hired two soloists for the funeral... Doves were released at the burial, and she had his body place in the mausoleum. His casket was transported by horse and carriage. It was by far the most extreme service that I had seen for an adult, let alone a still born baby.

Once that was over, I was really hoping that Violet could start to heal and move on with the rest of her life. She had a bright future and I wanted her to remember that. We donated all the baby stuff that she had bought to the Purple Heart, so she didn't have to keep being reminded of the tragedy. I made sure that I called and checked on her at least once a day.

"I just feel like I want to die," she said to me during one of our conversations.

"Don't say that. You have too much to live for," I said to her.

"No I don't. I don't have my son."

Everyday those words echoed in my head. All I wanted was for my sister to get back to normal. I missed the Violet that I had to put my hands on every now and then. I missed having our hilarious conversations. Now all we talked about was how miserable she was. I missed when my sister was happy. It's crazy how one event in our lives can turn us upside down.

I was no stranger to loss. I was no stranger to heartache or pain. I had been through many lows in my life. And I know I had only gotten through it by the grace of God. And now that I knew him for myself, I made sure I thanked Him for that. I couldn't wait for Violet to get to that level of understanding. She could get through this if she really wanted to. Sometimes we go through things and in some strange way we get comfortable with living in sorrow. We say we want to get out of it but we do nothing constructive to help us deal with what we are going through. I suggested grief counseling to her and she declined. So what did she want to do? Just lay around and be sad?

I started to feel like I was forcing myself on her and I didn't want to do that. So during another one of our short conversations I let her know that she didn't have to feel obligated to talk to me when I called. So the first day that she didn't answer, I thought nothing of it. But the second day of not talking to her didn't sit right with me. Something wasn't right. I could feel it. So I called Rochelle and let her know that we had to do a pop up visit to Violet's house. Of course she was down.

Rochelle met me over there, and we went into the building. I was nervous. My stomach had a sick feeling. Something was wrong.

"So you haven't heard nothing from her?" Rochelle asked as we walked down the hallway.

"Nope."

"Not even a text?"

"Not even a text."
"Well maybe she just don't wanna bothered," Rochelle suggested.
"She don't. But something is wrong. I feel it," I said.

We walked up to the door and I started to bang and ring the bell simultaneously. No answer. I pressed my ear against the door to see if I could hear anything. Nothing. I started to bang on the door again.
"Where's your key?" Rochelle asked.
"She took it back the last time she caught an attitude with me. You know how she do," I responded.

I was growing impatient and even more worried. I had been knocking for about five minutes and still no answer. I called her phone and it went straight to voice mail.
"V!" Open the door! Open the door!" I screamed at the door.

Still no answer. Something was not right. I knew she was in there, because her car was in the parking garage.
"Call 911. they can get us in there," said Rochelle.

I took her advice and called the police. I knew that I would have to make them feel like there was a valid reason for them to come out. So I told the operator about V's suicidal comments and how she had just had a still born baby and she had taken it pretty hard. They agreed to send help over and I continued to bang on the door. Still no response. At this point I was beside myself. I hadn't talked to my sister in two days. And given the compromised emotional state that she was in, anything could be going on in that condo. A few of her neighbors stepped out into the hallway, I guess to see what all the banging and yelling was about. But I didn't care.

Finally, two paramedics and three firefighters were coming down the hall.
"Thank God," I said aloud.

As soon as they approached me, I let them know what was going on. I didn't even give anybody the chance to ask. Rochelle just stood there silently.
"My little sister is in there. She has been very depressed and at times suicidal for the past two weeks. She gave birth to a still

born baby. So I need to get in there and make sure she is OK. I know she's in there her car is outside. But she's not answering any of my phone calls and that's not like her. Even when we are mad at each other she answers. I really think something is wrong," I explained to the fire fighter.
"So you think she may have hurt herself?" he asked.
"Yes. Yes I do," I said.

The second firefighter walked up to the door with an ax. "Do you know what type of locks she has on the door?" he asked.
"Yes. It's a deadbolt and a latch at the top," I informed him.
"OK. Stand back please."

Rochelle and I took a few steps back. He swung the ax and went right into the wall. He chopped away until finally there was a hole and you could see into Violet's condo. The firefighter without the ax stuck his hand in the whole and unlocked the door. He pulled his hand out and turned the knob. Bingo. We were in.
"Stay out here," one of them said to me.

After a few seconds, I couldn't take it anymore. The suspense was killing me. I barged my way in and Rochelle trailed behind me.
"Stay back!" the female paramedic said to me.

I pushed past her and stumbled into Violet's room. She was laying on the floor, and the other paramedic was by her side. She was unconscious.
"I knew it! I knew something was wrong!" I cried.

The firefighter who had used the ax to get us in grabbed me and got me out of the room. I was hysterical. I should've come to see about her sooner.
"Calm down," Rochelle said. "It's going to be alright."
"How? My sister is in there laying on the floor!"
"She's not dead. Her pulse is weak, but we're doing everything that we can. We just need you to stay calm," one of the other paramedics said to me.

They got V loaded up on the stretcher and we were on our way to the hospital. She had overdosed on pain medication and alcohol. There were pill bottles and empty bottles of gin scattered around her room. Again her words replayed in my head. I should've gotten her help as soon as she told me wanted to die. I slept on her comments and now look. I couldn't stomach having to call Aunt Lucy and tell her any more bad news, so I asked Rochelle to do it for me.

I was so relieved when the doctor let me know that Violet was stable and that she was going to make it. Glory to God. I could breathe a little now.

"Your Aunt said she wants you to call her when you get yourself together," Rochelle informed me.

"I'll call her tomorrow. I don't feel like answering a whole bunch of questions right now," I answered back.

"And you got a lot of missed calls from Brent."

I didn't even respond to that. I wasn't in the mood to talk to him either. I was mentally and emotionally worn out. He had been a bit needy ever since I had sex with him, and I honestly was starting to regret it. I had been avoiding his calls for the past week. I didn't have time for him at the moment. We went in to sit with Violet and she rolled her eyes at the sight of us. Didn't she have some nerve? How can you roll your eyes at the people who care about your life?

"I'm not going to talk you to death V. But I am going to say this. You need help. I want to be here for you, but you can not do this again. I love you... And I just need you to understand that you are not in this by yourself."

"I just feel like you were getting irritated when I didn't just bounce back right away. I feel like I don't have nobody who understands. That clown still won't answer none of my calls," Violet said.

"I know this is tough for you Violet. I just want you to come out of this. I know you can do it. I'm not irritated with you... I'm sad for you. That's all. It hurts me to see you like this. But I'm here. And I think the best thing for you to do is stop thinking about him, because he ain't thinking about you," I responded.

It was good that we got this conversation out of the

way. You had to be honest with the people that you loved. It was a must. I gave my sister a hug and sat back down. I looked over at Rochelle as she scrolled through her phone. There was a confused look on her face, then it quickly turned into shock.
"Oh my God," Rochelle said with wide eyes.
"What?" I inquired.
"I don't know if you really want to know."
"What?"
"You sure you want to know?"
"I mean not really if I don't need to."
"I think you need to," Rochelle said.
"Well what is it?" I asked again.
".... I don't know... Maybe this ain't the appropriate time."
"Would you just tell me?"
"OK... But don't get mad at me. TMZ got still shots of you and Brent," Rochelle replied.
"What?"

    Rochelle didn't say anything. She just handed me her phone. Sure enough there I was, on the balcony with Brent. My important parts that could be seen were blurred out, but what was going on was quite obvious. I felt like I was going to throw up. This wasn't good. All I could do was think of how many other people had seen it by now. My phone started to vibrate. It was Deon.
"Oh shit," I said.
"It's your husband ain't it?" Rochelle asked.

    I didn't answer her. I hit the cancel button and sent Deon to voice mail. I already knew what the call was about and I didn't want to hear it. Violet looked at me and shook her head.
"You let Brent smash?" she asked.
"Mind your business," I said.

    Violet chuckled a little. I'm glad she found it funny because I didn't. My life just couldn't be calm.

CHAPTER 22
Reflecting And Moving Forward

I got up the next morning knowing that I needed to hear a word from God. Deon had been ringing my phone off the hook and I knew things would get even worse once I got to the office on Monday morning. So on my way to church I drove in silence and I prayed. I needed some sort of peace in my life. It had been a roller coaster that year so far, and all I wanted was peace.

Once I arrived to church, I was greeted by a few members who didn't hesitate to ask where I had been. I told them briefly about how busy I was but the truth was I knew that I could have made time to get there. I got a few funny looks, and I wondered if they had seen the pictures that TMZ had released of Brent and I. Well, I wanted to be a big girl, so big girls had to deal with their consequences.

After some of the most beautiful singing from the choir and powerful liturgical dance from the praise team, it was time for offering. I hadn't paid my tithes since the last time I had been there. That was a shame. It would have been nothing for me to drop a check in the mail. I had to do better. I really did. I pulled out my check book and wrote a check for thirty thousand dollars, and sealed it in my envelope. I walked with my head held high all the way to the basket to dropped it in, even though I wanted to sink down and disappear. I was really disappointed in myself, and I wondered if God felt the same.

I sat back down and it was like a movie playing in my head. Being molested by Leon... The fight between him and my mother. Running to Virginia in the middle of the night... Having my first two kids in high school... Elaina and Franko betraying me... Franko getting killed... Moving to Baltimore and meeting Marlon... Having his wife come to the house... Finding out he was gay... Getting an abortion... Dancing at Showstoppers... Meeting Ra-Ra and having my house raided... Having him flip on me and become abusive... Meeting Deon... My mother dying... Finding out Leon wasn't my father... Me using drugs and tricking... Living out of motels... Being raped and almost beat to death... Overdosing... Stealing from Rochelle... Going to jail... Then Deon getting me out and life started to move upward... I got clean... Got my GED... Got my kids back... Got married... Then had Summer... Started a few businesses... Then more craziness... Bringing Violet to Baltimore... Baby Deon popping up... Running into Elaina... Trying to help her... Fighting Mocha.... Finding out Rochelle was having an affair with my brother in law... Deon cheating with the Nanny... Separating from Deon... Rochelle's brother being murdered...Taking Deon back and meeting my father... And then this year... Having all my business do extremely well... Then Deon tore his ACL and became dependent on pain killers...Aunt Lucinda being diagnosed with breast cancer... Trying to hold together a marriage that was breaking into pieces... While being a mom and mogul... Managing my sister while she is in the prime of her career only for her to get pregnant by a creep... Deon trying to make a move on my best friend... Separating from him again... Finding out about the craziness that went on between my father, mother, and Aunt... Almost slapping my brother's face off... Having Paul's wife who I knew nothing about walk in on us having a slightly personal, slightly business dinner... Man-Man almost dieing and me trying to patch things up with Deon AGAIN... Only to find out about another son that he never told me about and walking in on him and Trina getting close... Then sleeping with Brent on his balcony and having TMZ release pictures of it two weeks later... In the midst of my sister attempting suicide after having a still born baby... MY LIFE HAD BEEN ROUGH.

  Tears rolled down my cheeks and I didn't even bother to wipe them. I was damaged. I was damaged, but I was always trying to fix everyone else. I needed some time to fix myself. I focused back in on the service and my pastor was getting ready to preach. His message was coming from Psalm 110:1. The Lord said unto my Lord, sit thou at my right hand, until I make thine enemies thy footstool.

  The message was good, but I didn't feel like it was for me. Usually when I went to church, it was like the pastor was

preaching directly to me. But not this time. I wasn't mad though. There must've been some one there that needed to hear it. Before the benediction could even be given, my phone started buzzing. It was Deon. I sent him to the voice mail. I said, "see you next Sunday" to a few folks then I got out of there. I wanted to relax until I had to go pick up Summer from Rochelle. Miracle and Lil' Franko were at home being the laid back kids that they were. I got in my car and started it up. Once again my phone rang. I was pissed at this point.
"What do you want?"
"So you're mad and you think that fucking one of my team mates is gonna change something? All it did was make you look like a hoe," Deon insulted me.

    This man had changed. Well I don't know if he changed. Maybe he was always like that but he did his best to hide it in the beginning. There was another life lesson. A person's true colors will always show... Whether it's now, or later. And I was to the point where I was ready to accept it. Deon was a cheater. And he was disrespectful. He wasn't for me. And I wasn't going to continue to deal with a man who brought out the worst in me. I had to move forward.
"I don't care what you think about me Deon! I am going through too much to even think about you! Yes! I fucked Brent! So what? Ain't you over there with Trina?"

    I didn't give him a chance to respond. I ended that call. He wasn't worth my time, energy, or breath. And if his feelings were hurt, then good enough for him. Maybe now he could feel an ounce of what I felt after every time he betrayed me. I didn't owe him anything... Not even an explanation.

    I needed to clear my mind. It was like a million and one thoughts were going through my head. So I put my foot on the gas and drove to the one place that didn't upset me. My office. I pulled into my parking spot and I could see people standing at front of the building. A woman and children. Who could that be? Damn I need to go to the eye doctor and get some glasses! I got out of the car and walked toward the building. No one should've been here. Everybody knew that Lexi and I were not in the office on Sundays. The closer I got, the more apparent it became to me who it was.

"What are you doing here?" I asked her.

" I need your help," Elaina said.

"Hi Mrs. Clause," Hope said with a smile.

That's when the sermon became clear to me. I did need to hear it. The Bible says that He will make your enemy your footstool. The Bible is God's word, and God doesn't lie. So you get the picture. Hmmmmm... She needed my help huh? I knew she was gonna wind up needing me sooner or later. La Jefa to the rescue.

Made in the USA
Middletown, DE
07 September 2021